HIDDEN GIFTS

Hidden Gifts

*Finding Blessings
in the Struggles of Life*

Compiled by Brian Kurzius

Bahá'í
PUBLISHING
WILMETTE, ILLINOIS

Bahá'í Publishing
415 Linden Avenue, Wilmette, Illinois 60091-2844

Copyright © 2007 by the National Spiritual Assembly
of the Bahá'ís of the United States

All rights reserved. Published 2007
Printed in the United States of America on acid-free paper ∞

10   09   08   4   3   2

Library of Congress Cataloging-in-Publication Data
  Hidden gifts : finding blessings in the struggles of life / compiled by
Brian Kurzius.
     p. cm.
  Includes bibliographical references and index.
  ISBN-13: 978-1-931847-48-3 (alk. paper)
  ISBN-10: 1-931847-48-7 (alk. paper)
         1. Suffering—Religious aspects—Bahai Faith. I. Title.

BP388.S84K87 2007
297.9'3442—dc22

2007060817

Cover design by Robert A. Reddy

CONTENTS

INTRODUCTION / 1

WHY DO WE HAVE PROBLEMS? / 5
    For the Transformation of the Individual and Society / 6
    To Detach Us from Earthly Things / 14
    To Teach Us the Laws of Cause and Effect / 18

WHERE DO OUR PROBLEMS COME FROM? / 25
    From Ourselves / 25
    From Each Other / 32
    From the Material World / 36
    From Natural and Man-Made Disasters / 41
    Illness / 45
    Death / 49

HOW CAN WE COPE WITH OUR PROBLEMS? / 57
    Faith and Confidence / 57
    Determination and Discipline / 63
    Detachment / 72
    Patience, Contentment, and Gratitude / 76
    Prayer and Meditation / 85
    Overlooking the Faults of Others / 95
    Consulting with Others / 102
    Service to Others / 105

SELECTED PRAYERS / 113

NOTES / 121

BIBLIOGRAPHY / 131

INDEX / 135

For Christine, Jordan, and Shana

Hidden Gifts

INTRODUCTION

Every one of us—whether rich or poor, famous or unknown—has had our share of suffering. In response to these challenges we ponder and ask questions; we pray to God for answers or we look to psychology and philosophy to help us make sense of it all. Some of us avoid the questions altogether by drowning our troubles in drugs or alcohol. We may even deny the existence of God since we cannot conceive of a Creator who would allow innocent people to suffer.

My own approach to the study of suffering came not as an academic search but as an act of desperation. In my early twenties there came a point when I was overwhelmed by difficulties. Problems came from all sides—from physical and financial circumstances, from family and friends and, above all, as the result of my own actions. I questioned why people have cancer, die in earthquakes, or become victims of violent crime and I wondered if there *was* a God, why would He cause

INTRODUCTION

humans to suffer in this way. It seemed so unjust and unfair—and yet I *longed* to understand.

And so like many of us, I searched for answers. I looked everywhere—from seminars and self-help groups to books on psychology, philosophy, and religion—texts that dealt with the very nature of life and God.

Over time I found myself understanding suffering in a different way than before. I became less disturbed by the things that used to be intolerable and slowly began to proactively search for solutions to my difficulties.

Some of the books that were most helpful during this time included Harold Kushner's *When Bad Things Happen to Good People,* Victor Frankl's *Man's Search for Meaning,* M. Scott Peck's *The Road Less Traveled,* and other authors and speakers including Abraham Maslow, Leo Buscaglia, and John Bradshaw.

The focus of this compilation however is a selection of quotations which had the most profound effect on my finally coming to terms with the tests of life. These quotations—from the writings of the Bahá'í Faith*— offer a wealth of wisdom, guidance, and comfort on the subject of suffering. In addition to restating spiritual and philosophical truths, they also offer new approaches to age-old questions such as the meaning of life and the

---

* The Bahá'í Faith is an independent world religion that began in the middle of the nineteenth century and teaches the unity of all religions and the oneness of humanity. For more information please visit http://www.bahai.org.

INTRODUCTION

purpose of suffering—and suggest qualities we can develop to deal with all of life's challenges more effectively.

During the most difficult problems I have faced these writings have continuously inspired me to grow through my challenges. I sincerely hope that this book will provide you with the same measure of comfort, encouragement and appreciation for the gifts that are hidden in all the struggles of life.

WHY DO WE HAVE PROBLEMS?

To understand the value that difficulties serve in our lives—and the world at large—it seems that we first need to come to terms with the purpose of our lives on earth. Bahá'u'lláh,* the Prophet-Founder of the Bahá'í Faith, explained that although we are born into this world with a physical body, our true reality is spiritual. We are given a limited time on earth to prepare for our life in the next world—an existence that is purely spiritual. What we bring with us to the next world are not the material things we've gained. Instead, we take with us the spiritual qualities and virtues we have developed, such as love, patience, and self-discipline. This spiritual existence is also affected by the way we have been of service to others and made efforts to assist in the advancement of society.

---

* A brief introduction to the life of Bahá'u'lláh can be found at http://www.bahaullah.org/.

Why Do We Have Problems?

Our life on earth can therefore be seen as a kind of workshop, where the difficulties we face give us opportunities to develop spiritual qualities—such as being loving when others are unkind to us, or being truthful and trustworthy in a society that encourages lying and deceit. We are also given unnumbered chances to be of service to others.

For the Transformation of the Individual and Society

The Bahá'í writings explain that human beings have two natures. One is physical and the other is spiritual. The physical nature looks after its survival and is concerned primarily with its own material well-being. The spiritual nature, meanwhile, strives to manifest the attributes and qualities of God, such as love, kindness, patience, and contentment. Spiritual transformation is seen as the process of working to transcend our lower nature and the struggles we face are like the tests that we have in school. They allow us to check our progress and see the areas where we still need improvement.

Men who suffer not, attain no perfection. The plant most pruned by the gardeners is that one which, when the summer comes, will have the most beautiful blossoms and the most abundant fruit.¹

The more difficulties one sees in the world the more perfect one becomes. The more you plough and dig the ground the more fertile it becomes. The more you put the gold in the fire the purer it becomes. The more you sharpen the steel by grinding the better it cuts. Therefore, the more sorrows one sees the more perfect one becomes.²

Not until man is tried doth the pure gold distinctly separate from the dross. Torment is the fire of test wherein the pure gold shineth resplendently and the impurity is burned and blackened.³

Were it not for tests, pure gold could not be distinguished from the impure. Were it not for tests, the courageous could not be separated from the cowardly. Were it not for tests, the people of faithfulness could not be known from the disloyal. Were it not for tests, the intellectuals and the faculties of the scholars in great colleges would not develop. Were it not for tests, sparkling gems could not be known from worthless pebbles. Were it not for tests, nothing would progress in this contingent world.[4]

———•———

In the beginning of his human life man was embryonic in the world of the matrix. There he received capacity and endowment for the reality of human existence. The forces and powers necessary for this world were bestowed upon him in that limited condition. In this world he needed eyes; he received them potentially in the other. He needed ears; he obtained them there in readiness and preparation for his new existence. The powers requisite in this world were conferred upon him in the world of the matrix so that when he entered this realm of real existence he not only possessed all necessary functions and powers but found provision for his material sustenance awaiting him.

Therefore, in this world he must prepare himself for the life beyond. That which he needs in the world of the Kingdom must be obtained here. Just as he prepared himself in the world of the matrix by acquiring forces necessary in this sphere of existence, so, likewise, the indispensable forces of the divine existence must be potentially attained in this world.

What is he in need of in the Kingdom which transcends the life and limitation of this mortal sphere? That world beyond is a world of sanctity and radiance; therefore, it is necessary that in this world he should acquire these divine attributes. In that world there is need of spirituality, faith, assurance, the knowledge and love of God. These he must attain in this world so that after his ascension from the earthly to the heavenly Kingdom he shall find all that is needful in that eternal life ready for him.

That divine world is manifestly a world of lights; therefore, man has need of illumination here. That is a world of love; the love of God is essential. It is a world of perfections; virtues, or perfections, must be acquired. That world is vivified by the breaths of the Holy Spirit; in this world we must seek them. That is the Kingdom of everlasting life; it must be attained during this vanishing existence.

By what means can man acquire these things? How shall he obtain these merciful gifts and powers? First, through the knowledge of God. Second, through the love of God. Third, through faith. Fourth, through philanthropic deeds. Fifth, through self-sacrifice. Sixth, through severance from this world. Seventh, through sanctity and holiness. Unless he acquires these forces and attains to these requirements, he will surely be deprived of the life that is eternal. But if he possesses the knowledge of God, becomes ignited through the fire of the love of God, witnesses the great and mighty signs of the Kingdom, becomes the cause of love among mankind and lives in the utmost state of sanctity and holiness, he shall surely attain to second birth, be baptized by the Holy Spirit and enjoy everlasting existence.[5]

In man there are two natures; his spiritual or higher nature and his material or lower nature. In one he approaches God, in the other he lives for the world alone. Signs of both these natures are to be found in men. In his material aspect he expresses untruth, cruelty and injustice; all these are the outcome of his lower nature. The attributes of his Divine nature are shown forth in love, mercy, kindness, truth and justice, one and all being expressions of his higher nature. Every good habit, every noble quality belongs to man's spiritual nature, whereas all his imperfections and sinful actions are born of his material nature. If a man's Divine nature dominates his human nature, we have a saint.

Man has the power both to do good and to do evil; if his power for good predominates and his inclinations to do wrong are conquered, then man in truth may be called a saint. But if, on the contrary, he rejects the things of God and allows his evil passions to conquer him, then he is no better than a mere animal.[6]

Often physical sickness draws man nearer unto his Maker, suffers his heart to be made empty of all worldly desires until it becomes tender and sympathetic toward all sufferers and compassionate to all creatures. Although physical diseases cause man to suffer temporarily, yet they do not touch his spirit. Nay, rather, they contribute toward the divine purpose; that is, spiritual susceptibilities will be created in his heart.[7]

Could anything less than the fire of a civil war with all its violence and vicissitudes—a war that nearly rent the great American Republic—have welded the states, not only into a Union of independent units, but into a Nation, in spite of all the ethnic differences that characterized its component parts? . . . We have but to turn our gaze to humanity's blood-stained history to realize that nothing short of intense mental as well as physical agony has been able to precipitate those epoch-making changes that constitute the greatest landmarks in the history of human civilization. Great and far-reaching as have been those changes in the past, they cannot appear, when viewed in their proper perspective, except as subsidiary adjustments preluding that transformation of unparalleled majesty and scope which humanity is in this age bound to undergo. That the forces of a world catastrophe can alone precipitate such a new phase of human thought is, alas, becoming increasingly apparent.[8]

Physical pain is a necessary accompaniment of all human existence, and as such is unavoidable. As long as there will be life on earth, there will be also suffering, in various forms and degrees. But suffering, although an inescapable reality, can nevertheless be utilized as a means for the attainment of happiness. This is the interpretation given to it by all the prophets and saints who, in the midst of severe tests and trials, felt happy and joyous and experienced what is best and holiest in life. Suffering is both a reminder and a guide. It stimulates us better to adapt ourselves to our environmental conditions, and thus leads the way to self improvement. In every suffering one can find a meaning and a wisdom. But it is not always easy to find the secret of that wisdom. It is sometimes only when all our suffering has passed that we become aware of its usefulness. What man considers to be evil turns often to be a cause of infinite blessings. And this is due to his desire to know more than he can. God's wisdom is, indeed, inscrutable to us all, and it is no use pushing too far trying to discover that which shall always remain a mystery to our mind.[9]

[Difficulties] are the means of your spirit growing and developing. You will suddenly find that you have conquered many of the problems which upset you, and then you will wonder why they should have troubled you at all.[10]

The troubles of this world pass, and what we have left is what we have made of our souls, so it is to this we must look—to becoming more spiritual, drawing nearer to God, no matter what our human minds and bodies go through.[11]

We must always look ahead and seek to accomplish in the future what we may have failed to do in the past. Failures, tests, and trials, if we use them correctly, can become the means of purifying our spirit, strengthening our characters, and enable us to rise to greater heights of service.[12]

Suffering, of one kind or another, seems to be the portion of man in this world. Even the Beloved ones, the Prophets of God, have never been exempt from the ills that are to be found in our world; poverty, disease, bereavement—they seem to be part of the polish God employs to make us finer, and enable us to reflect more of His attributes![13]

To Detach Us from Earthly Things

Many times the problems in our lives are caused when we spend excessive amounts of time in the pursuit of material comforts while neglecting to develop our spiritual lives. We sometimes also disregard values such as truthfulness and honesty—even when our actions could hurt others—to advance our own well-being. Therefore, often the problems we face in life help us to realize that true happiness is best found not in our physical comforts, but rather in helping others and developing our spiritual qualities.

Know ye that by "the world" is meant your unawareness of Him Who is your Maker, and your absorption in aught else but Him. The "life to come," on the other hand, signifieth the things that give you a safe approach to God, the All-Glorious, the Incomparable. Whatsoever deterreth you, in this Day, from loving God is nothing but the world. Flee it, that ye may be numbered with the blest. Should a man wish to adorn himself with the ornaments of the earth, to wear its apparels, or partake of the benefits it can bestow, no harm can befall him, if he alloweth nothing whatever to intervene between him and God, for God hath ordained every good thing, whether created in the heavens or in the earth, for such of His servants as truly believe in Him. Eat ye, O people, of the good things which God hath allowed you, and deprive not yourselves from His wondrous bounties. Render thanks and praise unto Him, and be of them that are truly thankful.[14]

WHY DO WE HAVE PROBLEMS?

If we suffer it is the outcome of material things, and all the trials and troubles come from this world of illusion.

For instance, a merchant may lose his trade and depression ensues. A workman is dismissed and starvation stares him in the face. A farmer has a bad harvest, anxiety fills his mind. A man builds a house which is burnt to the ground and he is straightway homeless, ruined, and in despair.

All these examples are to show you that the trials which beset our every step, all our sorrow, pain, shame and grief, are born in the world of matter; whereas the spiritual Kingdom never causes sadness. A man living with his thoughts in this Kingdom knows perpetual joy. The ills all flesh is heir to do not pass him by, but they only touch the surface of his life, the depths are calm and serene.[15]

No comfort can be secured by any soul in this world, from monarch down to the most humble commoner. If once this life should offer a man a sweet cup, a hundred bitter ones will follow; such is the condition of this world. The wise man, therefore, doth not attach himself to this mortal life and doth not depend upon it; at some moments, even, he eagerly wisheth for death that he may thereby be freed from these sorrows and afflictions.[16]

The mind and spirit of man advance when he is tried by suffering. The more the ground is ploughed the better the seed will grow, the better the harvest will be. Just as the plough furrows the earth deeply, purifying it of weeds and thistles, so suffering and tribulation free man from the petty affairs of this worldly life until he arrives at a state of complete detachment. His attitude in this world will be that of divine happiness. Man is, so to speak, unripe: the heat of the fire of suffering will mature him. Look back to the times past and you will find that the greatest men have suffered most.[17]

Do not grieve at the afflictions and calamities that have befallen thee. All calamities and afflictions have been created for man so that he may spurn this mortal world—a world to which he is much attached. When he experienceth severe trials and hardships, then his nature will recoil and he will desire the eternal realm—a realm which is sanctified from all afflictions and calamities. Such is the case with the man who is wise. He shall never drink from a cup which is at the end distasteful, but, on the contrary, he will seek the cup of pure and limpid water. He will not taste of the honey that is mixed with poison.[18]

There is no human being untouched by these two influences [joy and pain]; but all the sorrow and the grief that exist come from the world of matter—the spiritual world bestows only the joy![19]

In the spiritual development of man a stage of purgation is indispensable, for it is while passing through it that the over-rated material needs are made to appear in their proper light . . . The present calamities are parts of this process of purgation, through them alone will man learn his lesson. They are to teach the nations that they have to view things internationally, they are to make the individual attribute more importance to his moral, than his material welfare.[20]

To Teach Us the Laws of Cause and Effect

The writings of the Bahá'í Faith explain that there are three types of laws in the world: man-made, physical, and spiritual. While physical laws—such as gravity—operate in the material world, spiritual laws govern our inner lives and can similarly cause problems for us if we disregard them.

For instance, if we are unkind to someone, and thus break the law of God to love each other, we will invariably suffer in some way. One negative consequence may be spiritual, such as feeling bad about our behavior and further away from God. But, should the person we were unkind to decide to retaliate, we may suffer a physical consequence as well.

The same process holds true for the world at large. So many of the problems in the world come from disregarding the fundamental unity of the human family. As we put into practice the spiritual laws of God—to treat others as we wish to be treated—all of our relationships, whether personal or among nations, will improve as a result.

It is incumbent upon them who are in authority to exercise moderation in all things. Whatsoever passeth beyond the limits of moderation will cease to exert a beneficial influence.[21]

In all matters moderation is desirable. If a thing is carried to excess, it will prove a source of evil.[22]

WHY DO WE HAVE PROBLEMS?

The tongue is a smoldering fire, and excess of speech a deadly poison. Material fire consumeth the body, whereas the fire of the tongue devoureth both heart and soul. The force of the former lasteth but for a time, whilst the effects of the latter endureth a century.[23]

The well-being of mankind, its peace and security, are unattainable unless and until its unity is firmly established.[24]

If a man eats too much, he ruins his digestion; if he takes poison he becomes ill or dies. If a person gambles he will lose his money; if he drinks too much he will lose his equilibrium. All these sufferings are caused by the man himself, it is quite clear therefore that certain sorrows are the result of our own deeds.[25]

Know thou that ordeals are of two kinds. One is for tests, and the other for punishment of misdeeds. That which is for testing is for one's education and development, and that which is for punishment of deeds is severe retribution.

TO TEACH US THE LAWS OF CAUSE AND EFFECT

The father and the teacher sometimes show tenderness towards the children and at other times deal harshly with them. Such severity is for educational purposes; it is true tenderness and absolute bounty and grace. Although in appearance it is wrath, in reality it is kindness. Although outwardly it is an ordeal, inwardly it is a cooling draught.[26]

The more we search for ourselves, the less likely we are to find ourselves; and the more we search for God, and to serve our fellow-men, the more profoundly will we become acquainted with ourselves, and the more inwardly assured. This is one of the great spiritual laws of life.[27]

Life is based on laws: physical, man-made, and spiritual. As you have broken the laws of the society in which you live, you will have to stand up like a man and take your punishment.* The spirit in which you do this is the most important thing, and constitutes a great opportunity for you. . . . Until your sentence is up, you must live within yourself in a way not to spoil the new

---

* This letter was written to a person who was in prison.

future awaiting you. You must not become bitter—for after all you are only reaping what you planted.[28]

———

Just as there are laws governing our physical lives, requiring that we must supply our bodies with certain foods, maintain them within a certain range of temperatures, and so forth, if we wish to avoid physical disabilities, so also there are laws governing our spiritual lives. These laws are revealed to mankind in each age by the Manifestation of God, and obedience to them is of vital importance if each human being, and mankind in general, is to develop properly and harmoniously. Moreover, these various aspects are interdependent. If an individual violates the spiritual laws for his own development he will cause injury not only to himself but to the society in which he lives.[29]

———

In considering the effect of obedience to the laws on individual lives, one must remember that the purpose of this life is to prepare the soul for the next. Here one must learn to control and direct one's animal impulses, not to be a slave to them. Life in this world is a succession of tests and achievements, of falling short and of making new spiritual advances. Sometimes the course may seem very hard, but one can witness, again and again, that the soul who steadfastly obeys the law of Bahá'u'lláh* however hard it may seem, grows spiritually, while the one who compromises with the law for the sake of his own apparent happiness is seen to have been following a chimera: he does not attain the happiness he sought, he retards his spiritual advance and often brings new problems upon himself.[30]

---

* In this context, obeying the "law of Bahá'u'lláh" is the same as obeying the laws of any of the Prophets of God such as Moses, Christ, and Muḥammad, all of whom brought divine teachings from God for the benefit of humanity.

WHERE DO OUR PROBLEMS COME FROM?

Identifying where a problem is coming from allows us to apply the proper solution. For example, if we automatically assume a difficulty we are facing is caused by someone else—when in reality it is the result of our own actions—we will be unable to correct our behavior and may go through the same situation at a later time.

It is like a doctor who needs to discover the cause of a disease in order to prescribe the proper remedy. No matter where our problems come from, they'll return again and again until we identify their source and work to resolve them once and for all.

From Ourselves

Sadly, we sometimes bring problems onto ourselves. When we do something that causes suffering to ourselves or others, it takes honesty and detachment to admit that we have made a mistake, see if we can do something to fix it, and determine to avoid repeating the error in the future. But at the same time, it is not helpful when we blame ourselves for things that we have no control over—nor should we burden ourselves with feelings of hopelessness and failure. We are like precious jewels that need to be inner beauty.

Therefore, the effort we make to overcome our weaknesses is often the most constructive thing we can do and can allow us to develop strengths that would otherwise not have been revealed.

Know, verily, that the soul is a sign of God, a heavenly gem whose reality the most learned of men hath failed to grasp, and whose mystery no mind, however acute, can ever hope to unravel. It is the first among all created things to declare the excellence of its Creator, the first to recognize His glory, to cleave to His truth, and to bow down in adoration before Him. If it be faithful to God, it will reflect His light, and will, eventually, return unto Him. If it fail, however, in its allegiance to its Creator, it will become a victim to self and passion, and will, in the end, sink in their depths.[1]

Indeed, man is noble, inasmuch as each one is a repository of the sign of God. Nevertheless, to regard oneself as superior in knowledge, learning or virtue, or to exalt oneself or seek preference, is a grievous transgression.[2]

Upon the reality of man . . . [God] hath focused the radiance of all of His names and attributes, and made it a mirror of His own Self. Alone of all created things man hath been singled out for so great a favor, so enduring a bounty.

These energies with which the Day Star of Divine bounty and Source of heavenly guidance hath endowed the reality of man lie, however, latent within him, even as the flame is hidden within the candle and the rays of light are potentially present in the lamp. The radiance of these energies may be obscured by worldly desires even as the light of the sun can be concealed beneath the dust and dross which cover the mirror. Neither the candle nor the lamp can be lighted through their own unaided efforts, nor can it ever be possible for the mirror to free itself from its dross. It is clear and evident that until a fire is kindled the lamp will never be ignited, and unless the dross is blotted out from the face of the mirror it can never represent the image of the sun nor reflect its light and glory.[3]

All men have been created to carry forward an ever-advancing civilization. The Almighty beareth Me witness: To act like the beasts of the field is unworthy of man. Those virtues that befit his dignity are forbearance, mercy, compassion and loving-kindness towards all the peoples and kindreds of the earth.[4]

Arise, O people, and, by the power of God's might, resolve to gain the victory over your own selves, that haply the whole earth may be freed and sanctified from its servitude to the gods of its idle fancies—gods that have inflicted such loss upon, and are responsible for the misery of, their wretched worshipers. These idols form the obstacle that impedeth man in his efforts to advance in the path of perfection. We cherish the hope that the Hand of Divine power may lend its assistance to mankind, and deliver it from its state of grievous abasement.[5]

Humility exalteth man to the heaven of glory and power, whilst pride abaseth him to the depths of wretchedness and degradation.[6]

Jealousy consumeth the body and anger doth burn the liver: avoid these two as you would a lion.[7]

Desire is a flame that has reduced to ashes uncounted lifetime harvests of the learned, a devouring fire that even the vast sea of their accumulated knowledge could never quench. How often has it happened that an individual who was graced with every attribute of humanity and wore the jewel of true understanding, nevertheless followed after his passions until his excellent qualities passed beyond moderation and he was forced into excess. His pure intentions changed to evil ones, his attributes were no longer put to uses worthy of them, and the power of his desires turned him aside from righteousness and its rewards into ways that were dangerous and dark. A good character is in the sight of God and His chosen ones and the possessors of insight, the most excellent and praiseworthy of all things, but always on condition that its center of emanation should be reason and knowledge and its base should be true moderation.[8]

The root cause of wrongdoing is ignorance, and we must therefore hold fast to the tools of perception and knowledge. Good character must be taught. Light must be spread afar, so that, in the school of humanity, all may acquire the heavenly characteristics of the spirit, and see for themselves beyond any doubt that there is no fiercer hell, no more fiery abyss, than to possess a character that is evil and unsound; no more darksome pit nor loathsome torment than to show forth qualities which deserve to be condemned.

The individual must be educated to such a high degree that he would rather have his throat cut than tell a lie, and would think it easier to be slashed with a sword or pierced with a spear than to utter calumny or be carried away by wrath.

Thus will be kindled the sense of human dignity and pride.[9]

Know that there are two kinds of torment: subtle and gross. For example, ignorance itself is a torment, but it is a subtle torment; indifference to God is itself a torment; so also are falsehood, cruelty and treachery. All the imperfections are torments, but they are subtle torments. Certainly for an intelligent man death is better than sin, and a cut tongue is better than lying or calumny. The other kind of torment is gross—such as penalties, imprisonment, beating, expulsion and banishment. But for the people of God separation from God is the greatest torment of all.[10]

The complete and entire elimination of the ego would imply perfection—which man can never completely attain—but the ego can and should be ever-increasingly subordinated to the enlightened soul of man. This is what spiritual progress implies.[11]

Life is a constant struggle, not only against forces around us, but above all against our own ego. We can never afford to rest on our own oars, for if we do, we soon see ourselves carried down stream again. . . . Sometimes, of course, people fail because of a test they just do not meet, and often our severest tests come from each other.[12]

The only people who are truly free of the "dross of self" are the Prophets, for to be free of one's ego is a hall-mark of perfection. We humans are never going to become perfect, for perfection belongs to a realm we are not destined to enter. However, we must constantly mount higher, seek to be more perfect.

The ego is the animal in us, the heritage of the flesh which is full of selfish desires. By obeying the laws of God, seeking to live the life laid down in our teachings, and prayer and struggle, we can subdue our egos. We call people "saints" who have achieved the highest degree of mastery over their egos.[13]

From Each Other

Some of the difficulties we face are caused by the actions of others and can be even more challenging if they include personal attacks or if we are not in a position to avoid the people we are having troubles with. No matter how others may treat us, it is important to realize that we always have the ability to choose how we respond. We should make every effort to avoid condemning others, as none of us can truly judge the actions of another. It can also be helpful to spend as much time as possible with friends who can help us see our problems in a positive light. Not only will these types of friendships assist and encourage us to become better people—we in turn can encourage our friends!

Today all people are immersed in the world of nature. That is why thou dost see jealousy, greed, the struggle for survival, deception, hypocrisy, tyranny, oppression, disputes, strife, bloodshed, looting and pillaging, which all emanate from the world of nature. Few are those who have been freed from this darkness, who have ascended from the world of nature to the world of man, who have followed the divine Teachings, have served the world of humanity, are resplendent, merciful, illumined and like unto a rose garden. Strive thine utmost to become godlike, characterized with His attributes, illumined and merciful, that thou mayest be freed from every bond and become attached at heart to the Kingdom of the incomparable Lord.[14]

Consider how the Prophets Who have been sent, the great souls who have appeared and the sages who have arisen in the world have exhorted mankind to unity and love. This has been the essence of their mission and teaching. This has been the goal of their guidance and message. The Prophets, saints, seers and philosophers have sacrificed their lives in order to establish these principles and teachings amongst men. Consider the heedlessness of the world, for notwithstanding the efforts and sufferings of the Prophets of God, the nations and peoples are still engaged in hostility and fighting.

Notwithstanding the heavenly commandments to love one another, they are still shedding each other's blood. How heedless and ignorant are the people of the world! How gross the darkness which envelops them! Although they are the children of a compassionate God, they continue to live and act in opposition to His will and good pleasure. God is loving and kind to all men, and yet they show the utmost enmity and hatred toward each other. God is the Giver of life to them, and yet they constantly seek to destroy life. God blesses and protects their homes; they rage, sack and destroy each other's homes. Consider their ignorance and heedlessness![15]

As regards the questions of young children and of weak, defenseless souls who are afflicted at the hand of the oppressor, in this a great wisdom is concealed. The question is one of cardinal importance, but briefly it may be stated that in the world to come a mighty recompense awaiteth such souls. Much, indeed, might be said upon this theme, and upon how the afflictions that they bear in life become cause for them of such an outpouring of Divine mercy and bestowal as is preferable to a hundred thousand comforts and to a world of growth and development in this transitory abode.[16]

There are persons with whom you associate and converse whose utterances are life-imparting, joy-giving. The withered and faded are refreshed, the joyless become happy, the extinct become enkindled and the lifeless are quickened with the breaths of the Holy Spirit. The one drowned in the sea of hesitation and doubt is saved by the life-boat of certainty and assurance; the one attached to this material world becomes severed and the one steeped in blameworthy deeds is adorned with praiseworthy attributes. On the other hand there are some persons whose very respiration extinguishes the light of faith.[17]

To be approved of God alone should be one's aim.

When God calls a soul to a high station, it is because that soul has capacity for that station as a gift of God, and because that soul has supplicated to be taken into His service. No envies, jealousies, calumnies, slanders, plots, nor schemes will ever move God to remove a soul from its intended place, for by the grace of God, such actions on the part of the people are the test of the servant, testing his strength, forbearance, endurance and sincerity under adversity. At the same time those who show forth envies, jealousies, etc., toward a servant, are depriving themselves of their own stations, and not another of his, for they prove by their own acts that they are not only unworthy of being called to any station awaiting them, but also prove that they cannot withstand the very first test—that of rejoicing over the success of their neighbor, at which God rejoices. Only by such a sincere joy can the gift of God descend into a pure heart.[18]

The principal cause of this suffering, which one can witness wherever one turns, is the corruption of human morals and the prevalence of prejudice, suspicion, hatred, untrustworthiness, selfishness and tyranny among men. It is not merely material well-being that people need. What they desperately need is to know how to live their lives—they need to know who they are, to what purpose they exist, and how they should act towards one another; and, once they know the answers to these questions they need to be helped to gradually apply these answers to everyday behavior. It is to the solution of this basic problem of mankind that the greater part of all our energy and resources should be directed.[19]

From the Material World

Another source of our problems is the world and its material concerns. If we have very little money, for instance, many of our challenges will revolve around the daily struggle to pay for the basic requirements of life. But we also find that when we are surrounded by the comforts of life we can easily forget the sufferings of others and become self-satisfied and complacent regarding the things of the spirit. Bahá'u'lláh taught that while enjoying the benefits and blessings of this world, we should be careful that excessive attention to our material desires doesn't distract us from the daily effort also needed to develop our spiritual qualities and assist in the advancement of the world around us.

Be not troubled in poverty nor confident in riches, for poverty is followed by riches, and riches are followed by poverty.[20]

O ye that pride yourselves on mortal riches! Know ye in truth that wealth is a mighty barrier between the seeker and his desire, the lover and his beloved. The rich, but for a few, shall in no wise attain the court of His presence nor enter the city of content and resignation. Well is it then with him, who, being rich, is not hindered by his riches from the eternal kingdom, nor deprived by them of imperishable dominion.[21]

Mortal charm shall fade away, roses shall give way to thorns, and beauty and youth shall live their day and be no more.[22]

———·———

Every soul seeketh an object and cherisheth a desire, and day and night striveth to attain his aim. One craveth riches, another thirsteth for glory and still another yearneth for fame, for art, for prosperity and the like. Yet finally all are doomed to loss and disappointment. One and all they leave behind them all that is theirs and empty-handed hasten to the realm beyond, and all their labors shall be in vain. To dust they shall all return, denuded, depressed, disheartened and in utter despair.[23]

———·———

Woe and misery to the soul that seeketh after comforts, riches, and earthly delights while neglecting to call God to mind![24]

———·———

Some men's lives are solely occupied with the things of this world; their minds are so circumscribed by exterior manners and traditional interests that they are blind to any other realm of existence, to the spiritual significance of all things! They think and dream of earthly fame, of material progress. Sensuous delights and comfortable surroundings bound their horizon, their highest ambitions center in successes of worldly conditions and circumstances! They curb not their lower propensities; they eat, drink, and sleep! Like the animal, they have no thought beyond their own physical well-being. It is true that these necessities must be dispatched. Life is a load which must be carried on while we are on earth, but the cares of the lower things of life should not be allowed to monopolize all the thoughts and aspirations of a human being. The heart's ambitions should ascend to a more glorious goal, mental activity should rise to higher levels! Men should hold in their souls the vision of celestial perfection, and there prepare a dwelling-place for the inexhaustible bounty of the Divine Spirit.

Let your ambition be the achievement on earth of a Heavenly civilization! I ask for you the supreme blessing, that you may be so filled with the vitality of the Heavenly Spirit that you may be the cause of life to the world.[25]

Wealth has a tempting and drawing quality. It bewilders the sight of its charmed victims with showy appearances and draws them on and on to the edge of yawning chasms. It makes a person self-centered, self-occupied, forgetful of God and of holy things.[26]

The chief reason for the evils now rampant in society is the lack of spirituality. The materialistic civilization of our age has so much absorbed the energy and interest of mankind that people in general do no longer feel the necessity of raising themselves above the forces and conditions of their daily material existence. There is not sufficient demand for things that we should call spiritual to differentiate them from the needs and requirements of our physical existence. The universal crisis affecting mankind is, therefore, essentially spiritual in its causes. The spirit of the age, taken on the whole, is irreligious. Man's outlook on life is too crude and materialistic to enable him to elevate himself into the higher realms of the spirit.[27]

It would be perhaps impossible to find a nation or people not in a state of crisis today. The materialism, the lack of true religion and the consequent baser forces in human nature which are being released, have brought the whole world to the brink of probably the greatest crisis it has ever faced or will have to face.[28]

One of the signs of a decadent society, a sign which is very evident in the world today, is an almost frenetic devotion to pleasure and diversion, an insatiable thirst for amusement, a fanatical devotion to games and sport, a reluctance to treat any matter seriously, and a scornful, derisory attitude towards virtue and solid worth. . . .

Frivolity palls and eventually leads to boredom and emptiness, but true happiness and joy and humor that are parts of a balanced life that includes serious thought, compassion and humble servitude to God, are characteristics that enrich life and add to its radiance.[29]

From Natural and Man-Made Disasters

Some of the most difficult challenges we can face are those that occur as a result of natural and man-made disasters. Regardless of their cause—whether from the uncontrolled forces of nature, the acts of other humans, or simply by accident or chance—they all hold the potential to not only bring about the transformation of the individual but also the collective life of humanity.

Chaos and confusion are daily increasing in the world. They will attain such intensity as to render the frame of mankind unable to bear them. Then will men be awakened and become aware that religion is the impregnable stronghold and the manifest light of the world, and its laws, exhortations and teachings the source of life on earth.[30]

God has created men to love each other; but instead, they kill each other with cruelty and bloodshed. God has created them that they may cooperate and mingle in accord; but instead, they ravage, plunder and destroy in the carnage of battle. God has created them to be the cause of mutual felicity and peace; but instead, discord, lamentation and anguish rise from the hearts of the innocent and afflicted.[31]

Those were indeed dire events in San Francisco.* Disasters of this kind should serve to awaken the people, and

---

* The earthquake of 1906.

diminish the love of their hearts for this inconstant world. It is in this nether world that such tragic things take place: this is the cup that yieldeth bitter wine.[32]

There is a tremendous darkness in the world today, the darkness caused by mankind's going against the Laws of God and giving way to the animal side of human nature.[33]

When . . . a crisis sweeps over the world no person should hope to remain intact. We belong to an organic unit and when one part of the organism suffers all the rest of the body will feel its consequence.[34]

The Bahá'í approach to resolution of the manifold problems affecting human society rests upon the assertion by Bahá'u'lláh that these ills are but various symptoms and side effects of the basic disease, which the Divine Physician has diagnosed to be disunity. Bahá'u'lláh has made it abundantly clear that the first step essential for the health and harmony of the whole of mankind is its unification. He says, "The well-being of mankind, its peace and security are unattainable unless and until its unity is firmly established." By contrast, the approach of most people is the exact opposite: their concentration is on attempts to remedy the multitude of ills besetting mankind, with the expectation that the resolution of these problems will lead ultimately to unity.[35]

Every discerning eye clearly sees that the early stages of this chaos have daily manifestations affecting the structure of human society; its destructive forces are uprooting time-honored institutions which were a haven and refuge for the inhabitants of the earth in bygone days and centuries, and around which revolved all human affairs. The same destructive forces are also deranging the political, economic, scientific, literary, and moral equilibrium of the world and are destroying the fairest fruits of the present civilization. Political machinations of those in authority have placed the seal of obsolescence upon the root principles of the world's order. Greed and passion, deceit, hypocrisy, tyranny, and pride are dominating features afflicting human relations. Discoveries and inventions, which are the fruit of scientific and technological advancements, have become the means and tools of mass extermination and destruction.[36]

Illness

Dealing with illness can be tremendously difficult—whether the sickess is our own or that of a friend or loved one. And while some illnesses can be cured through proper diet, exercise, or medical treatment, others may continue for years and cause us to wonder what possible benefit they serve. The Bahá'í writings explain that while we should do everything we can to take care of our health, when we become ill we should seek the assistance of doctors at the same time as we take advantage of spiritual means of healing such as the use of prayer and meditation. We can also derive comfort from the knowledge that our spirit is always close to God regardless of our physical condition, and that at some point in our lives the gifts hidden within these challenges may also become clear to us.

Know thou that the soul of man is exalted above, and is independent of all infirmities of body or mind. That a sick person showeth signs of weakness is due to the hindrances that interpose themselves between his soul and his body, for the soul itself remaineth unaffected by any bodily ailments.[37]

Although ill health is one of the unavoidable conditions of man, truly it is hard to bear. The bounty of good health is the greatest of all gifts.[38]

Unless the spirit be healed, the cure of the body is worth nothing. All is in the hands of God, and without Him there can be no health in us![39]

Illnesses which occur by reason of physical causes should be treated by doctors with medical remedies; those which are due to spiritual causes disappear through spiritual means. Thus an illness caused by affliction, fear, nervous impressions, will be healed more effectively by spiritual rather than by physical treatment. Hence, both kinds of treatment should be followed; they are not contradictory. Therefore thou shouldst also accept physical remedies inasmuch as these too have come from the mercy and favor of God, Who hath revealed and made manifest medical science so that His servants may profit from this kind of treatment also. Thou shouldst give equal attention to spiritual treatments, for they produce marvelous effects.[40]

It is incumbent upon everyone to seek medical treatment and to follow the doctor's instructions, for this is in compliance with the divine ordinance, but, in reality, He Who giveth healing is God.[41]

With regard to your question concerning spiritual healing. Such a healing constitutes, indeed, one of the most effective methods of relieving a person from either his mental or physical pains and sufferings. . . . Spiritual healing, however, is not and cannot be a substitute for material healing, but it is a most valuable adjunct to it. Both are, indeed, essential and complementary.[42]

Physical healing cannot be complete and lasting unless it is reinforced by spiritual healing.[43]

It is very hard to be subject to any illness, particularly a mental one. However, we must always remember these illnesses have nothing to do with our spirit or our inner relation to God. It is a great pity that as yet so little is really known of the mind, its workings and the illnesses that afflict it; no doubt, as the world becomes more spiritually minded and scientists understand the true nature of man, more humane and permanent cures for mental diseases will be found. . . .

You must always remember, no matter how much you or others may be afflicted with mental troubles and the crushing environment of these State Institutions, that your spirit is healthy, near to our Beloved, and will in the next world enjoy a happy and normal state of soul. Let us hope in the meantime scientists will find better and permanent cures for the mentally afflicted. But in this world such illness is truly a heavy burden to bear![44]

Mental illness is not spiritual, although its effects may indeed hinder and be a burden in one's striving toward spiritual progress.[45]

The best results for the healing process are to combine the spiritual with the physical, for it should be possible for you to overcome your illness through the combined and sustained power of prayer and of determined effort.[46]

Death

The Bahá'í writings explain that we should not fear death, but rather live our daily lives in the knowledge that we will take with us the good qualities we have developed in this world when we move on to the next stage of our existence. But certainly when we contemplate our own death—or deal with the death of a loved one—it can be the cause of some of our most heartbreaking struggles.

Know thou of a truth that the soul, after its separation from the body, will continue to progress until it attaineth the presence of God, in a state and condition which neither the revolution of ages and centuries, nor the changes and chances of this world, can alter. It will endure as long as the Kingdom of God, His sovereignty, His dominion and power will endure. It will manifest the signs of God and His attributes, and will reveal His loving kindness and bounty. The movement of My Pen is stilled when it attempteth to befittingly describe the loftiness and glory of so exalted a station. The honor with which the Hand of Mercy will invest the soul is such as no tongue can adequately reveal, nor any other earthly agency describe.[47]

The death of that beloved youth and his separation from you have caused the utmost sorrow and grief; for he winged his flight in the flower of his age and the bloom of his youth to the heavenly nest. But he hath been freed from this sorrow-stricken shelter and hath turned his face toward the everlasting nest of the Kingdom, and, being delivered from a dark and narrow world, hath hastened to the sanctified realm of light; therein lieth the consolation of our hearts.

The inscrutable divine wisdom underlieth such heart-rending occurrences. It is as if a kind gardener transferreth a fresh and tender shrub from a confined place to a wide open area. This transfer is not the cause of the withering, the lessening or the destruction of that shrub; nay, on the contrary, it maketh it to grow and thrive, acquire freshness and delicacy, become green and bear fruit. This hidden secret is well known to the gardener, but those souls who are unaware of this bounty suppose that the gardener, in his anger and wrath, hath uprooted the shrub.

Yet to those who are aware, this concealed fact is manifest, and this predestined decree is considered a bounty. Do not feel grieved or disconsolate, therefore, at the ascension of that bird of faithfulness; nay, under all circumstances pray for that youth, supplicating for him forgiveness and the elevation of his station.[48]

These human conditions [of passing on to the next world] may be likened to the matrix of the mother from which a child is to be born into the spacious outer world. At first the infant finds it very difficult to reconcile itself to its new existence. It cries as if not wishing to be separated from its narrow abode and imagining that life is restricted to that limited space. It is reluctant to leave its home, but nature forces it into this world. Having come into its new conditions, it finds that it has passed from darkness into a sphere of radiance; from gloomy and restricted surroundings it has been transferred to a spacious and delightful environment. Its nourishment was the blood of the mother; now it finds delicious food to enjoy. Its new life is filled with brightness and beauty; it looks with wonder and delight upon the mountains, meadows and fields of green, the rivers and fountains, the wonderful stars; it breathes the life-quickening atmosphere; and then it praises God for its release from the confinement of its former condition and attainment to the freedom of a new realm. This analogy expresses the relation of the temporal world to the life hereafter—the transition of the soul of man from darkness and uncertainty to the light and reality of the eternal Kingdom. At first it is very difficult to welcome death, but after attaining its new condition the soul is grateful, for it has been released from the bondage of the limited to enjoy the liberties of the unlimited. It has been freed from a world of sorrow, grief and trials to live in a world of unending bliss and joy. The phenomenal and physical have been abandoned in order that it may attain the opportunities of the ideal and spiritual. Therefore, the souls of those who have passed away from earth and completed their span of mortal pilgrimage . . . have hastened to a world superior to this. They have soared away from these conditions of darkness and dim vision into the realm of light. These are the only considerations which can comfort and console those whom they have left behind.[49]

DEATH

To consider that after the death of the body the spirit perishes is like imagining that a bird in a cage will be destroyed if the cage is broken, though the bird has nothing to fear from the destruction of the cage. Our body is like the cage, and the spirit is like the bird. We see that without the cage this bird flies in the world of sleep; therefore, if the cage becomes broken, the bird will continue and exist. Its feelings will be even more powerful, its perceptions greater, and its happiness increased. In truth, from hell it reaches a paradise of delights because for the thankful birds there is no paradise greater than freedom.[50]

When the human soul soareth out of this transient heap of dust and riseth into the world of God, then veils will fall away, and verities will come to light, and all things unknown before will be made clear, and hidden truths be understood.

Consider how a being, in the world of the womb, was deaf of ear and blind of eye, and mute of tongue; how he was bereft of any perceptions at all. But once, out of that world of darkness, he passed into this world of light, then his eye saw, his ear heard, his tongue spoke. In the same way, once he hath hastened away from this mortal place into the Kingdom of God, then he will be born in the spirit; then the eye of his perception will open, the ear of his soul will hearken, and all the truths of which he was ignorant before will be made plain and clear.[51]

Do not grieve, and do not lament. That tender and lovely shrub has been transferred from this world to the rose-garden of the Kingdom and that longing dove has flown to the divine nest. That candle has been extinguished in this nether world that it may be rekindled in the Supreme Concourse. Ye shall assuredly meet him face to face in the world of mysteries at the assemblage of Light.[52]

In the next world, man will find himself freed from many of the disabilities under which he now suffers. Those who have passed on through death, have a sphere of their own. It is not removed from ours; their work, the work of the Kingdom, is ours; but it is sanctified from what we call "time and place." Time with us is measured by the sun. When there is no more sunrise, and no more sunset, that kind of time does not exist for man. Those who have ascended have different attributes from those who are still on earth, yet there is no real separation.

"In prayer there is a mingling of station, a mingling of condition. Pray for them as they pray for you!"[53]

If you have a bed of lilies of the valley that you love and tenderly care for, they cannot see you, nor can they understand your care, nevertheless, because of that tender care, they flourish.

So it is with your husband. You cannot see him, but his loving influence surrounds you, cares for you, watches over you. They, who have passed into the Divine Garden, pray for us there, as we pray for them here.[54]

Such earnest souls, when they pass out of this life, enter a state of being far nobler and more beautiful than this one. We fear it only because it is unknown to us and we have little faith in the words of the Prophets who bring a true message of certainty from that realm of the spirit. We should face death with joy especially if our life upon this plane of existence has been full of good deeds.[55]

The progress of the soul does not come to an end with death. It rather starts along a new line. . . . Spiritual progress in that realm is infinite, and no man, while on this earth, can visualize its full power and extent.[56]

HOW CAN WE COPE WITH OUR PROBLEMS?

When we are in the midst of our problems how do we find the hidden gifts within them? How do we not only succeed in passing our tests but actually transform them into blessings?

We find that throughout history the people who have contributed most to the advancement of society have suffered great hardships in their lives. Instead of giving up or complaining about their trials, they have been able to turn their stumbling blocks into stepping stones.

We can do the same thing. By developing our spiritual qualities and strengths, not only will we benefit from our struggles, but also can be the source of comfort and assistance to others who face similar challenges.

Faith and Confidence

Faith and confidence enable us to have a sense of trust that things will work out well in the end. They help us to see the end in the beginning—to know that despite all outward appearances the challenges that we face will re-

veal their blessings to us eventually. These qualities also provide us with a calm assurance that God will come to our assistance in the hour of our greatest need.

Be not afraid of anyone, place thy whole trust in God, the Almighty, the All-Knowing.[1]

Place not thy reliance on thy treasures. Put thy whole confidence in the grace of God, thy Lord. Let Him be thy trust in whatever thou doest, and be of them that have submitted themselves to His Will.[2]

Whatever hath befallen you, hath been for the sake of God. This is the truth, and in this there is no doubt. You should, therefore, leave all your affairs in His Hands, place your trust in Him, and rely upon Him. He will assuredly not forsake you. In this, likewise, there is no doubt. No father will surrender his sons to devouring beasts; no shepherd will leave his flock to ravening wolves. He will most certainly do his utmost to protect his own. If, however, for a few days, in compliance with God's all-encompassing wisdom, outward affairs should run their course contrary to one's cherished desire, this is of no consequence and should not matter. Our intent is that all the friends should fix their gaze on the Supreme Horizon, and cling to that which hath been revealed in the Tablets.[3]

Rid thou thyself of all attachments to aught except God, enrich thyself in God by dispensing with all else besides Him, and recite this prayer:

> Say: God sufficeth all things above all things, and nothing in the heavens or in the earth or in whatever lieth between them but God, thy Lord, sufficeth. Verily, He is in Himself the Knower, the Sustainer, the Omnipotent.
>
> Regard not the all-sufficing power of God as an idle fancy. It is that genuine faith which thou cherishest for the Manifestation of God in every Dispensation. It is such faith which sufficeth above all the things that exist on the earth, whereas no created thing on earth besides faith would suffice thee.[4]

Indeed, if God willeth, He is potent to turn the stone into a mirror, but the person himself remaineth reconciled to his state. Had he wished to become a crystal, God would have made him to assume crystal form.[5]

———

Be ye assured and confident that the confirmations of God are descending upon you, the assistance of God will be given unto you, the breaths of the Holy Spirit will quicken you with a new life.[6]

———

O thou who art turning thy face towards God! Close thine eyes to all things else, and open them to the realm of the All-Glorious. Ask whatsoever thou wishest of Him alone; seek whatsoever thou seekest from Him alone. With a look He granteth a hundred thousand hopes, with a glance He healeth a hundred thousand incurable ills, with a nod He layeth balm on every wound, with a glimpse He freeth the hearts from the shackles of grief. He doeth as He doeth, and what recourse have we? He carrieth out His Will, He ordaineth what He pleaseth. Then better for thee to bow down thy head in submission, and put thy trust in the All-Merciful Lord.[7]

———

Never lose thy trust in God. Be thou ever hopeful, for the bounties of God never cease to flow upon man. If viewed from one perspective they seem to decrease, but from another they are full and complete. Man is under all conditions immersed in a sea of God's blessings. Therefore, be thou not hopeless under any circumstances, but rather be firm in thy hope.[8]

True happiness depends on spiritual good and having the heart ever open to receive the Divine Bounty.

If the heart turns away from the blessings God offers how can it hope for happiness? If it does not put its hope and trust in God's Mercy, where can it find rest? Oh, trust in God! for His Bounty is everlasting, and in His Blessings, for they are superb. Oh! put your faith in the Almighty, for He faileth not and His goodness endureth for ever! His Sun giveth Light continually, and the Clouds of His Mercy are full of the Waters of Compassion with which He waters the hearts of all who trust in Him.[9]

When a man has faith, all the mountains of the world cannot turn him back. No, he will endure any trial, any disaster, and nothing will weaken him. But one who is not a true believer, one who lacks real faith, will lament over the least disappointment, and cry out against the slightest thing which mars his peace and pleasure.[10]

———•———

Through the light of faith the darkness which envelops our thoughts and feelings gives way to a radiance and a splendor before which every gloom vanishes.[11]

———•———

Naturally there will be periods of distress and difficulty, and even severe tests, but if that person turns firmly toward the divine Manifestation, studies carefully His spiritual teachings and receives the blessings of the Holy Spirit, he will find that in reality these tests and difficulties have been the gifts of God to enable him to grow and develop.[12]

———•———

There are . . . innumerable examples of individuals who have been able to effect drastic and enduring changes in their behavior, through drawing on the spiritual powers available by the bounty of God.[13]

———•———

Determination and Discipline

Determination and discipline help us to fight against the natural inertia that can set in when we are overwhelmed by our struggles, and to forge ahead in the midst of our severest trials. We also find that when we are fully resolved and determined to attain a specific goal in life, the confidence and energy required come as a matter of course.

Success or failure, gain or loss, must . . . depend upon man's own exertions. The more he striveth, the greater will be his progress.[14]

———

All that which ye potentially possess can, however, be manifested only as a result of your own volition. Your own acts testify to this truth.[15]

———

[God] will never deal unjustly with any one, neither will He task a soul beyond its power. He, verily, is the Compassionate, the All-Merciful.[16]

Yield not to grief and sorrow; they cause the greatest misery.[17]

———•———

Be thou strong and firm. Be thou resolute and steadfast. When the tree is firmly rooted, it will bear fruit. Therefore, it is not permitted to be agitated by any test. Be thou not disheartened. Be thou not discouraged. The trials of God are many, but if man remains firm and steadfast, test itself is a stepping stone for the progress of humanity.[18]

———•———

The beloved of the Lord must stand fixed as the mountains, firm as impregnable walls. Unmoved must they remain by even the direst adversities, ungrieved by the worst of disasters. Let them cling to the hem of Almighty God, and put their faith in the Beauty of the Most High; let them lean on the unfailing help that cometh from the Ancient Kingdom, and depend on the care and protection of the generous Lord. Let them at all times refresh and restore themselves with the dews of heavenly grace, and with the breaths of the Holy Spirit revive and renew themselves from moment to moment.[19]

———•———

DETERMINATION AND DISCIPLINE

When a thought of war comes, oppose it by a stronger thought of peace. A thought of hatred must be destroyed by a more powerful thought of love.[20]

The happiness and greatness, the rank and station, the pleasure and peace, of an individual have never consisted in his personal wealth, but rather in his excellent character, his high resolve, the breadth of his learning, and his ability to solve difficult problems.[21]

Man must travel in the way of God. Day by day he must endeavor to become better, his belief must increase and become firmer, his good qualities and his turning to God must be greater, the fire of his love must flame more brightly; then day by day he will make progress, for to stop advancing is the means of going back. The bird when he flies soars ever higher and higher, for as soon as he stops flying he will come down. Every day, in the morning when arising you should compare today with yesterday and see in what condition you are. If you see your belief is stronger and your heart more occupied with God and your love increased and your freedom from the world greater then thank God and ask for the increase of these qualities. You must begin to pray and repent for all that you have done which is wrong and you must implore and ask for help and assistance that you may become better than yesterday so that you may continue to make progress.[22]

Man is a child of God, most noble, lofty and beloved by God, his Creator. Therefore, he must ever strive that the divine bounties and virtues bestowed upon him may prevail and control him. Just now the soil of human hearts seems like black earth, but in the innermost substance of this dark soil there are thousands of fragrant flowers latent. We must endeavor to cultivate and awaken these potentialities, discover the secret treasure in this very mine and depository of God, bring forth these resplendent powers long hidden in human hearts. Then will the glories of both worlds be blended and increased and the quintessence of human existence be made manifest.[23]

What profit is there in agreeing that universal friendship is good, and talking of the solidarity of the human race as a grand ideal? Unless these thoughts are translated into the world of action, they are useless.

DETERMINATION AND DISCIPLINE

The wrong in the world continues to exist just because people talk only of their ideals, and do not strive to put them into practice. If actions took the place of words, the world's misery would very soon be changed into comfort.[24]

We are living in a day of reliance upon material conditions. Men imagine that the great size and strength of a ship, the perfection of machinery or the skill of a navigator will ensure safety, but these disasters* sometimes take place that men may know that God is the real Protector. If it be the will of God to protect man, a little ship may escape destruction, whereas the greatest and most perfectly constructed vessel with the best and most skillful navigator may not survive a danger such as was present on the ocean. The purpose is that the people of the world may turn to God, the One Protector; that human souls may rely upon His preservation and know that He is the real safety. These events happen in order that man's faith may be increased and strengthened. Therefore, although we feel sad and disheartened, we must supplicate God to turn our hearts to the Kingdom and pray for these departed souls with faith in His infinite

---

* The sinking of the Titanic in 1912.

mercy so that, although they have been deprived of this earthly life, they may enjoy a new existence in the supreme mansions of the Heavenly Father.

    Let no one imagine that these words imply that man should not be thorough and careful in his undertakings. God has endowed man with intelligence so that he may safeguard and protect himself. Therefore, he must provide and surround himself with all that scientific skill can produce. He must be deliberate, thoughtful and thorough in his purposes, build the best ship and provide the most experienced captain; yet, withal, let him rely upon God and consider God as the one Keeper. If God protects, nothing can imperil man's safety; and if it be not His will to safeguard, no amount of preparation and precaution will avail.[25]

The children must be carefully trained to be most courteous and well-behaved. They must be constantly encouraged and made eager to gain all the summits of human accomplishment, so that from their earliest years they will be taught to have high aims, to conduct themselves well, to be chaste, pure, and undefiled, and will learn to be of powerful resolve and firm of purpose in all things. Let them not jest and trifle, but earnestly advance unto

DETERMINATION AND DISCIPLINE

their goals, so that in every situation they will be found resolute and firm.[26]

———•———

Man must be tireless in his effort. Once his effort is directed in the proper channel if he does not succeed today, he will succeed tomorrow. Effort in itself is one of the noblest traits of human character. Devotion to one's calling, effort in its speedy execution, simplicity of spirit and steadfastness through all the ups and downs, these are the hallmarks of success. A person characterized with these attributes will gather the fruits of his labors and will win the happiness of the kingdom.[27]

———•———

Without firmness there will be no result, Trees must be firm in the ground to give fruit. The foundation of a building must be very solid in order to support the building. If there be the slightest doubt in a believer, he will be without result. How often did Christ warn Peter to be steadfast! Therefore, consider how difficult it is to remain firm, especially in the time of trials. If man endure and overcome the trials, the more will he become firm and steadfast. When the tree is firmly rooted, the more the wind blows the more the tree will benefit; the more intense the wind the greater the benefit. But if weak, it will immediately fall.[28]

———•———

Each of us must improve himself, that he may attain nothing short of the best. When one stops, he descends. A bird, when it is flying, soars; but as soon as it stops, it falls. While man is directed upward, he develops. As soon as he stops, he descends. . . .

There exist in man two powers. One power uplifts him. This is divine attraction, which causes man's elevation. In all grades of existence he will develop through this power. This belongs to the spirit. The other power causes man to descend. This is the animal nature. The first attracts man to the Kingdom. The second brings him down to the contingent world. Now we must consider which of these will gain more power. If the heavenly power overcome, man will become heavenly, enlightened, merciful; but if the worldly power overcome, he will be dark, satanic, and like the animal. Therefore he must develop continually. As long as the heavenly power is the great force, man will ascend.[29]

———•———

DETERMINATION AND DISCIPLINE

Perfection of work is man's greatest reward. When a man sees his work perfected and this perfection is the result of incessant labor and application he is the happiest man in the world. Work is the source of human happiness.[30]

———

There are certain forms of work which are beyond human endurance and others which are within it; and these differ according to the early environment and training of each individual. . . . The struggling, winning, successful man is he who accustoms himself to the accomplishment of those things which are considered to be beyond human endurance. Only a soul thus great can stand the tests of life and come out of the crucible pure and unspotted.[31]

———

Our past is not the thing that matters so much in this world as what we intend to do with our future. The inestimable value of religion is that when a man is vitally connected with it, through a real and living belief in it and in the Prophet Who brought it, he receives a strength greater than his own which helps him to develop his good characteristics and overcome his bad ones. The whole purpose of religion is to change not only our thoughts but our acts; when we believe in God and His Prophet and His Teachings, we are growing, even though we perhaps thought ourselves incapable of growth and change![32]

Detachment

While God has created the many blessings of the material world for us to enjoy, we should avoid being so attached to them that we forget our spiritual natures—or the challenges being faced by the people around us. Being detached from our problems and from the material things of the world also helps us to be more flexible and accepting when things happen in our lives that we don't expect.

The world is but a show, vain and empty, a mere nothing, bearing the semblance of reality. Set not your affections upon it. Break not the bond that uniteth you with your Creator, and be not of those that have erred and strayed from His ways. Verily I say, the world is like the vapor in a desert, which the thirsty dreameth to be water and striveth after it with all his might, until when he cometh unto it, he findeth it to be mere illusion.[33]

DETACHMENT

Should prosperity befall thee, rejoice not, and should abasement come upon thee, grieve not, for both shall pass away and be no more.[34]

O thou handmaid aflame with the fire of God's love! Grieve thou not over the troubles and hardships of this nether world, nor be thou glad in times of ease and comfort, for both shall pass away. This present life is even as a swelling wave, or a mirage, or drifting shadows. Could ever a distorted image on the desert serve as refreshing waters? No, by the Lord of Lords! Never can reality and the mere semblance of reality be one, and wide is the difference between fancy and fact, between truth and the phantom thereof.

Know thou that the Kingdom is the real world, and this nether place is only its shadow stretching out. A shadow hath no life of its own; its existence is only a fantasy, and nothing more; it is but images reflected in water, and seeming as pictures to the eye.[35]

Wherefore dwell thou ever in the Kingdom, and be thou oblivious of this world below. Be thou so wholly absorbed in the emanations of the spirit that nothing in the world of man will distract thee.[36]

Stay ye entirely clear of this dark world's concerns, and become ye known by the attributes of those essences that make their home in the Kingdom. Then shall ye see how intense is the glory of the heavenly Day-Star, and how blinding bright are the tokens of bounty coming out of the invisible realm.[37]

Let us not keep on forever with our fancies and illusions, with our analyzing and interpreting and circulating of complex dubieties. Let us put aside all thoughts of self; let us close our eyes to all on earth, let us neither make known our sufferings nor complain of our wrongs. Rather let us become oblivious of our own selves, and drinking down the wine of heavenly grace, let us cry out our joy, and lose ourselves in the beauty of the All-Glorious.[38]

DETACHMENT

The more one is severed from the world, from desires, from human affairs, and conditions, the more impervious does one become to the tests of God. Tests are a means by which a soul is measured as to its fitness, and proven out by its own acts. God knows its fitness beforehand, and also its unpreparedness, but man, with an ego, would not believe himself unfit unless proof were given him . . . and the tests are continued until the soul realizes its own unfitness, then remorse and regret tend to root out the weakness.[39]

Whenever you see tremendous personal problems in your private lives . . . you must remember that these afflictions are part of human life; and, according to our teachings one of their wisdoms is to teach us the impermanence of this world and the permanence of the spiritual bonds that we establish with God, His Prophet, and those who are alive in the faith of God. You must always remember that the Manifestations of God, Themselves, were not immune to suffering of the most human nature; and that from the hands of their relatives, they drank the bitterest potions. . . . Beside their afflictions, our afflictions, however terrible for us, must seem small in comparison.[40]

Patience, Contentment, and Gratitude

The qualities of patience, contentment, and gratitude are closely related to detachment. Developing these qualities helps us to realize that despite the problems we may be facing there are innumerable things for which we can be grateful. When we focus on the positive side of things, it can help us to get through seemingly impossible trials.

Be generous in your days of plenty, and be patient in the hour of loss. Adversity is followed by success and rejoicings follow woe.[41]

Blessed are the steadfastly enduring, they that are patient under ills and hardships, who lament not over anything that befalleth them, and who tread the path of resignation.[42]

Sorrow not if, in these days and on this earthly plane, things contrary to your wishes have been ordained and manifested by God, for days of blissful joy, of heavenly delight, are assuredly in store for you. Worlds, holy and spiritually glorious, will be unveiled to your eyes. You are destined by Him, in this world and hereafter, to partake of their benefits, to share in their joys, and to obtain a portion of their sustaining grace. To each and every one of them you will, no doubt, attain.[43]

The virtues and attributes pertaining unto God are all evident and manifest, and have been mentioned and described in all the heavenly Books. Among them are trustworthiness, truthfulness, purity of heart while communing with God, forbearance, resignation to whatever the Almighty hath decreed, contentment with the things His Will hath provided, patience, nay, thankfulness in the midst of tribulation, and complete reliance, in all circumstances, upon Him. These rank, according to the estimate of God, among the highest and most laudable of all acts.[44]

The source of all glory is acceptance of whatsoever the Lord hath bestowed, and contentment with that which God hath ordained. . . .

The essence of true safety is to observe silence, to look at the end of things and to renounce the world.[45]

———

Concerning thine own affairs, if thou wouldst content thyself with whatever might come to pass it would be praiseworthy. To engage in some profession is highly commendable, for when occupied with work one is less likely to dwell on the unpleasant aspects of life.[46]

———

There was once a lover who had sighed for long years in separation from his beloved, and wasted in the fire of remoteness. From the rule of love, his heart was empty of patience, and his body weary of his spirit; he reckoned life without her as a mockery, and time consumed him away. How many a day he found no rest in longing for her; how many a night the pain of her kept him from sleep; his body was worn to a sigh, his heart's wound had turned him to a cry of sorrow. He had given a thousand lives for one taste of the cup of her presence, but it availed him not. The doctors knew no cure for him, and companions avoided his company; yea, physicians have no medicine for one sick of love, unless the favor of the beloved one deliver him.

PATIENCE, CONTENTMENT, AND GRATITUDE

At last, the tree of his longing yielded the fruit of despair, and the fire of his hope fell to ashes. Then one night he could live no more, and he went out of his house and made for the marketplace. On a sudden, a watchman followed after him. He broke into a run, with the watchman following; then other watchmen came together, and barred passage to the weary one. And the wretched one cried from his heart, and ran here and there, and moaned to himself: "Surely this watchman is 'Izrá'íl, my angel of death, following so fast upon me; or he is a tyrant of men, seeking to harm me." His feet carried him on, the one bleeding with the arrow of love, and his heart lamented. Then he came to a garden wall, and with untold pain he scaled it, for it proved very high; and forgetting his life, he threw himself down to the garden.

And there he beheld his beloved with a lamp in her hand, searching for a ring she had lost. When the heart-surrendered lover looked on his ravishing love, he drew a great breath and raised up his hands in prayer, crying: "O God! Give Thou glory to the watchman, and riches and long life. For the watchman was Gabriel, guiding this poor one; or he was Israfil, bringing life to this wretched one!"

Indeed, his words were true, for he had found many a secret justice in this seeming tyranny of the watchman, and seen how many a mercy lay hid behind the veil. Out of wrath, the guard had led him who was athirst in love's desert to the sea of his loved one, and lit up the dark night of absence with the light of reunion. He had driven one who was afar, into the garden of nearness, had guided an ailing soul to the heart's physician.

Now if the lover could have looked ahead, he would have blessed the watchman at the start, and prayed on his behalf, and he would have seen that tyranny as justice; but since the end was veiled to him, he moaned and made his plaint in the beginning. Yet those who journey in the garden land of knowledge, because they see the end in the beginning, see peace in war and friendliness in anger.[47]

By self-surrender and perpetual union with God is meant that men should merge their will wholly in the Will of God, and regard their desires as utter nothingness beside His Purpose. Whatsoever the Creator commandeth His creatures to observe, the same must they diligently, and with the utmost joy and eagerness, arise and fulfill. They should in no wise allow their fancy to obscure their judgment, neither should they regard their own imaginings as the voice of the Eternal. . . . In this consisteth the complete surrender of one's will to the Will of God.[48]

Every night is followed by a day, and every day has a night. Every spring has an autumn, and every autumn has its spring.[49]

Joy gives us wings! In times of joy our strength is more vital, our intellect keener, and our understanding less clouded. We seem better able to cope with the world and to find our sphere of usefulness. But when sadness visits us we become weak, our strength leaves us, our comprehension is dim and our intelligence veiled. The actualities of life seem to elude our grasp, the eyes of our spirits fail to discover the sacred mysteries, and we become even as dead beings.[50]

This material world of ours is a world of contrasts. It has in itself abundance and destitution, joy and sorrow, youth and old age. It is all the time changing and one has to undergo these different stages. Hence it behooves every faithful person to be patient and to be grateful for that which he receives.

It is fitting for those in the Kingdom to be satisfied with their fate and look only toward the increase of the heavenly spark in their hearts for this, alone, will give them rest and consolation. And you, too, should endeavor to increase that spiritual flame, known as the love of God, for through its increase you will enter into a new world of love and contentment. . . .

Be comforted, and trust in the mercy of the Merciful One, for it is said, "He who is not contented with what he receives, let him seek a God other than Me."[51]

We should not be occupied with our failings and weaknesses, but concern ourselves with the will of God so that it may flow through us, thereby healing these human infirmities.[52]

When one is released from the prison of self, that is, indeed, freedom! For self is the greatest prison.

When this release takes place, one can never be imprisoned. Unless one accepts dire vicissitudes, not with dull resignation, but with radiant acquiescence, one cannot attain this freedom.[53]

Man must live in contentment with the conditions of his time. He must not make himself the slave of any habit. He must eat a piece of stale bread with the same relish and enjoyment as the most sumptuous dinner. Contentment is real wealth. If one develops within himself the quality of contentment he will become independent. Contentment is the creator of happiness. When one is contented he does not care either for riches or poverty. He lives above the influence of them and is indifferent to them.[54]

We must not only be patient with others, infinitely patient!, but also with our own poor selves, remembering that even the Prophets of God sometimes got tired and cried out in despair![55]

Life afflicts us with very severe trials sometimes, but we must always remember that when we accept patiently the Will of God He compensates us in other ways. With faith and love we must be patient, and He will surely reward us.[56]

Do not feel discouraged if your labors do not always yield an abundant fruitage. For a quick and rapidly-won success is not always the best and the most lasting.[57]

———•———

As we almost never attain any spiritual goal without seeing the next goal we must attain still beyond our reach, he urges you, who have come so far already on the path of spirituality, not to fret about the distance you still have to cover! It is an indefinite journey, and, no doubt in the next world the soul is privileged to draw closer to God than is possible when bound on this physical plane.[58]

———•———

Self-sacrifice means to subordinate this lower nature and its desires to the more godly and noble side of our selves. Ultimately, in its highest sense, self-sacrifice means to give our will and our all to God to do with as He pleases. Then He purifies and glorifies our true self until it becomes a shining and wonderful reality.[59]

Prayer and Meditation

Just as we need food to maintain our physical bodies, daily prayer and meditation are essential for a healthy spiritual life. Prayer helps us to find peace within our hearts and meditation allows us to contemplate our problems and to find creative solutions to resolve them. They also help to open our hearts to the power of intuition, which, although it can't be relied on as an infallible source of guidance, may from time to time keep us from doing something that would cause difficulty—or inspire us with a new way to solve our problems.

Peruse ye every day the verses revealed by God. Blessed is the man who reciteth them and reflecteth upon them. He truly is of them with whom it shall be well.[60]

The remembrance of [God] is a healing medicine to the hearts of such as have drawn nigh unto Thy court.[61]

Whoso reciteth, in the privacy of his chamber, the verses revealed by God, the scattering angels of the Almighty shall scatter abroad the fragrance of the words uttered by his mouth, and shall cause the heart of every righteous man to throb. Though he may, at first, remain unaware of its effect, yet the virtue of the grace vouchsafed unto him must needs sooner or later exercise its influence upon his soul.[62]

Gather ye together with the utmost joy and fellowship and recite the verses revealed by the merciful Lord. By so doing the doors to true knowledge will be opened to your inner beings, and ye will then feel your souls endowed with steadfastness and your hearts filled with radiant joy.[63]

If sorrow and adversity visit us, let us turn our faces to the Kingdom and heavenly consolation will be outpoured.

If we are sick and in distress let us implore God's healing, and He will answer our prayer.

When our thoughts are filled with the bitterness of this world, let us turn our eyes to the sweetness of God's compassion and He will send us heavenly calm![64]

Pray for strength. It will be given to you, no matter how difficult the conditions.[65]

The prayers which were revealed to ask for healing apply both to physical and spiritual healing. Recite them, then, to heal both the soul and the body. If healing is right for the patient, it will certainly be granted; but for some ailing persons, healing would only be the cause of other ills, and therefore wisdom doth not permit an affirmative answer to the prayer.[66]

God will answer the prayer of every servant if that prayer is urgent. His mercy is vast, illimitable. He answers the prayers of all His servants. . . .

But we ask for things which the divine wisdom does not desire for us, and there is no answer to our prayer. His wisdom does not sanction what we wish. We pray, "O God! Make me wealthy!" If this prayer were universally answered, human affairs would be at a standstill. There would be none left to work in the streets, none to till the soil, none to build, none to run the trains. Therefore, it is evident that it would not be well for us if all prayers were answered. The affairs of the world would be interfered with, energies crippled and progress hindered. But whatever we ask for which is in accord with divine wisdom, God will answer. Assuredly!

For instance, a very feeble patient may ask the doctor to give him food which would be positively dangerous to his life and condition. He may beg for roast meat. The doctor is kind and wise. He knows it would be dangerous to his patient so he refuses to allow it. The doctor is merciful; the patient, ignorant. Through the doctor's kindness the patient recovers; his life is saved. Yet the patient may cry out that the doctor is unkind, not good, because he refuses to answer his pleading.

God is merciful. In His mercy He answers the prayers of all His servants when according to His supreme wisdom it is necessary.[67]

The progress of man's spirit in the divine world, after the severance of its connection with the body of dust, is through the bounty and grace of the Lord alone, or through the intercession and the sincere prayers of other human souls, or through the charities and important good works which are performed in its name.[68]

As we have power to pray for these souls here, so likewise we shall possess the same power in the other world, which is the Kingdom of God. Are not all the people in that world the creatures of God? Therefore, in that world also they can make progress. As here they can receive light by their supplications, there also they can plead for forgiveness and receive light through entreaties and supplications. Thus as souls in this world, through the help of the supplications, the entreaties and the prayers of the holy ones, can acquire development, so is it the same after death.[69]

Through the faculty of meditation man attains to eternal life; through it he receives the breath of the Holy Spirit—the bestowal of the Spirit is given in reflection and meditation.

The spirit of man is itself informed and strengthened during meditation; through it affairs of which man knew nothing are unfolded before his view. Through it he receives Divine inspiration, through it he receives heavenly food....

This faculty of meditation frees man from the animal nature, discerns the reality of things, puts man in touch with God.[70]

There is no doubt that the forces of the higher worlds interplay with the forces of this plane. The heart of man is open to inspiration; this is spiritual communication. As in a dream one talks with a friend while the mouth is silent, so is it in the conversation of the spirit.[71]

Sincere prayer always has its effect, and it has a great influence in the other world. We are never cut off from those who are there. The real and genuine influence is not in this world but in that other.[72]

The true worshiper, while praying, should endeavor not so much to ask God to fulfill his wishes and desires, but rather to adjust these and make them conform to the Divine Will. Only through such an attitude can one derive that feeling of inner peace and contentment which the power of prayer alone can confer.[73]

Regarding your question about prayer and the fact that some of our problems are not solved through prayer, we must always realize that life brings to us many situations, some of which are tests sent from God to train our characters, some of which are accidental conditions because we live in the world of nature and are subject to the accidents of death, disease, etc., and some of which we bring on ourselves by folly, selfishness or some other human trait.

It is not correct to say that because a loved one dies, or is not cured of a disease, or a problem is not solved, that God did not answer our prayer, or that we did not pray to Him in a way to receive a favorable answer. Maybe what we prayed for was not the Will of God or was the result of an accident and it produced an irrevocable conclusion like death or disease or bankruptcy.[74]

Peace of mind is gained by the centering of the spiritual consciousness on the Prophet of God; therefore you should study the spiritual Teachings, and receive the Water of Life from the Holy Utterances. Then by translating these high ideals into action, your entire character will be changed, and your mind will not only find peace, but your entire being will find joy and enthusiasm.[75]

You should not neglect your health, but consider it the means which enables you to serve. It—the body—is like a horse which carries the personality and spirit, and as such should be well cared for so it can do its work! You should certainly safeguard your nerves, and force yourself to take time, and not only for prayer and meditation, but for real rest and relaxation.[76]

Prayer alone is not sufficient. To render it more effective we have to make use of all the physical and material advantages which God has given us. Healing through purely spiritual forces is undoubtedly as inadequate as that which materialist physicians and thinkers vainly seek to obtain by resorting entirely to mechanical devices and methods. The best result can be obtained by combining the two processes, spiritual and physical.[77]

Five Steps of Prayer—Suggestions to solve problems with prayer and meditation

First Step. Pray and meditate about it. Use the prayers of the Manifestations as they have the greatest power. Then remain in the silence of contemplation for a few minutes.

Second Step. Arrive at a decision and hold to this. This decision is usually born during the contemplation. It may seem almost impossible of accomplishment but if it seems to be an answer to a prayer or a way of solving the problem, then immediately take the next step.

Third Step. Have determination to carry the decision through. Many fail here. The decision, budding into determination, is blighted and instead becomes a wish or a vague longing. When determination is born, immediately take the next step.

Fourth Step. Have faith and confidence that the power will flow through you, the right way will appear, the door will open, the right book will be given too you. Have confidence, and the right thing will come to your need. Then, as you rise from prayer, take at once the fifth step.

Fifth Step. Act as though it had all been answered. Act with tireless, ceaseless energy. And as you act, you, yourself, will become a magnet, which will attract more power to your being, until you become an unobstructed channel for the Divine Power to flow through you. Many pray but do not remain for the last half of the first step. Some who meditate arrive at a decision, but fail to hold it. Few have the determination of carry the decision through, and still fewer have the confidence that the right thing will come to their need. But how many remember to act as though it had all been answered? How true are those words—"Greater than the prayer is the spirit in which it is uttered, but greater than the way it is uttered is the spirit in which it is carried out."[78]

Such hindrances [illness and outer difficulties] no matter how severe and insuperable they may at first seem, can and should be effectively overcome through the combined and sustained power of prayer and of determined and continued effort.[79]

Overlooking the Faults of Others

Learning to forgive and forget—and to become so confident within ourselves that we do not allow others to make us unhappy—brings tremendous blessings into our lives. It helps us to appreciate the struggles of others and to recognize that each one of us has our own tests to face. In addition, since the most difficult people to deal with are often those who have had the most serious problems in their lives, empathy and compassion can bring great healing both to our hearts and our relationships with others.

If the fire of self overcome you, remember your own faults and not the faults of My creatures, inasmuch as every one of you knoweth his own self better than he knoweth others.[80]

If ye become aware of a sin committed by another, conceal it, that God may conceal your own sin.[81]

If others hurl their darts against you, offer them milk and honey in return; if they poison your lives, sweeten their souls; if they injure you, teach them how to be comforted; if they inflict a wound upon you, be a balm to their sores; if they sting you, hold to their lips a refreshing cup.[82]

———•———

One must see in every human being only that which is worthy of praise. When this is done, one can be a friend to the whole human race. If, however, we look at people from the standpoint of their faults, then being a friend to them is a formidable task. . . .

Thus is it incumbent upon us, when we direct our gaze toward other people, to see where they excel, not where they fail.[83]

———•———

Let your thoughts dwell on your own spiritual development, and close your eyes to the deficiencies of other souls. Act ye in such wise, showing forth pure and goodly deeds, and modesty and humility, that ye will cause others to be awakened.[84]

———•———

Never speak disparagingly of others, but praise without distinction. Pollute not your tongues by speaking evil of another. Recognize your enemies as friends, and consider those who wish you evil as the wishers of good. You must not see evil as evil and then compromise with your opinion, for to treat in a smooth, kindly way one whom you consider evil or an enemy is hypocrisy, and this is not worthy or allowable. You must consider your enemies as your friends, look upon your evil-wishers as your well-wishers and treat them accordingly. Act in such a way that your heart may be free from hatred. Let not your heart be offended with anyone. If some one commits an error and wrong toward you, you must instantly forgive him. Do not complain of others. Refrain from reprimanding them, and if you wish to give admonition or advice, let it be offered in such a way that it will not burden the bearer. Turn all your thoughts toward bringing joy to hearts. Beware! Beware! lest ye offend any heart. Assist the world of humanity as much as possible. Be the source of consolation to every sad one, assist every weak one, be helpful to every indigent one, care for every sick one, be the cause of glorification to every lowly one, and shelter those who are overshadowed by fear.[85]

Beware lest ye harm any soul, or make any heart to sorrow; lest ye wound any man with your words, be he known to you or a stranger, be he friend or foe. Pray ye for all; ask ye that all be blessed, all be forgiven.[86]

If two souls quarrel and contend about a question of the divine questions, differing and disputing, both are wrong. The wisdom of this incontrovertible law of God is this: That between two souls from amongst the believers of God, no contention and dispute may arise; that they may speak with each other with infinite amity and love.[87]

All mankind are the servants of the glorious God, our Creator. He has created all. Assuredly He must have loved them equally; otherwise, He would not have created them. He protects all. Assuredly He loves His creatures; otherwise, He would not protect them. He provides for all, proving His love for all without distinction or preference. He manifests His perfect goodness and lovingkindness toward all. He does not punish us for our sins and shortcomings, and we are all immersed in the ocean of His infinite mercy. Inasmuch as God is clement and loving to His children, lenient and merciful toward our shortcomings, why should we be unkind and unforgiving toward each other?[88]

Every aggressor deprives himself of God's grace. It is incumbent upon everyone to show the utmost love, rectitude of conduct, straightforwardness and sincere kindliness unto all the peoples and kindreds of the world, be they friends or strangers.[89]

Strive with all your power to be free from imperfections. Heedless souls are always seeking faults in others. What can the hypocrite know of others' faults when he is blind to his own? . . . As long as a man does not find his own faults, he can never become perfect. Nothing is more fruitful for man than the knowledge of his own shortcomings.[90]

All religions teach that we should love one another; that we should seek out our own shortcomings before we presume to condemn the faults of others, that we must not consider ourselves superior to our neighbors! We must be careful not to exalt ourselves lest we be humiliated.

Who are we that we should judge? How shall we know who, in the sight of God, is the most upright man? God's thoughts are not like our thoughts! How many men who have seemed saint-like to their friends have fallen into the greatest humiliation. Think of Judas Iscariot; he began well, but remember his end! On the other hand, Paul, the Apostle, was in his early life an enemy of Christ, whilst later he became His most faithful servant. How then can we flatter ourselves and despise others?

Let us therefore be humble, without prejudices, preferring others' good to our own! Let us never say, "I am a believer but he is an infidel," "I am near to God, whilst he is an outcast." We can never know what will be the final judgment! Therefore let us help all who are in need of any kind of assistance.

Let us teach the ignorant, and take care of the young child until he grows to maturity. When we find a person fallen into the depths of misery or sin we must be kind to him, take him by the hand, help him to regain his footing, his strength; we must guide him with love and tenderness, treat him as a friend not as an enemy.

OVERLOOKING THE FAULTS OF OTHERS

We have no right to look upon any of our fellow-mortals as evil.[91]

———·———

The truth is, nothing is sweeter for a man than doing good to someone who has done evil to him. Whenever he remembers having been kind to his enemies, his heart will rejoice.[92]

———·———

Love is, indeed, a most potent elixir that can transform the vilest and meanest of people into heavenly souls.[93]

———·———

We must love God, and in this state, a general love for all men becomes possible. We cannot love each human being for himself but our feeling towards humanity should be motivated by our love for the Father who created all men.[94]

———·———

Each of us is responsible for one life only, and that is our own. Each of us is immeasurably far from being "perfect as our heavenly father is perfect" and the task of perfecting our own life and character is one that requires all our attention, our will-power and energy. If we allow our attention and energy to be taken up in efforts to keep others right and remedy their faults, we are wasting precious time. We are like ploughmen each of whom has his team to manage and his plough to direct, and in order to keep his furrow straight he must keep his eye on his goal and concentrate on his own task. If he looks to this side and that to see how Tom and Harry are getting on and to criticize their ploughing, then his own furrow will assuredly become crooked.[95]

Consulting with Others

When we are in the midst of a problem it can be very hard to see clearly enough to formulate a solution. Consultation, whether we discuss issues with a friend, a doctor, or one who is an expert in a particular field (such as consulting with an accountant if we have problems with finances), provides a fresh perspective—allowing us to see our challenge from a different angle. An even greater benefit can be found through group consultation where several people together help to uncover solutions that none individually might have considered.

∽ ∽ ∽

The heaven of divine wisdom is illumined with the two luminaries of consultation and compassion. Take ye counsel together in all matters, inasmuch as consultation is the lamp of guidance which leadeth the way, and is the bestower of understanding.[96]

No welfare and no well-being can be attained except through consultation.[97]

Consultation bestows greater awareness and transmutes conjecture into certitude. It is a shining light which, in a dark world, leads the way and guides. For everything there is and will continue to be a station of perfection and maturity. The maturity of the gift of understanding is made manifest through consultation.[98]

Settle all things, both great and small, by consultation. Without prior consultation, take no important step in your own personal affairs.[99]

———•·•———

The purpose of consultation is to show that the views of several individuals are assuredly preferable to one man, even as the power of a number of men is of course greater than the power of one man.[100]

———•·•———

The question of consultation is of the utmost importance, and is one of the most potent instruments conducive to the tranquillity and felicity of the people. For example, when a believer is uncertain about his affairs, or when he seeketh to pursue a project or trade, the friends should gather together and devise a solution for him. He, in his turn, should act accordingly. Likewise in larger issues, when a problem ariseth, or a difficulty occurreth, the wise should gather, consult, and devise a solution. They should then rely upon the one true God, and surrender to His Providence, in whatever way it may be revealed, for divine confirmations will undoubtedly assist.[101]

Service to Others

The best remedy to many of our problems is to find some way to be of service to others. Not only can our struggles help us to become more sympathetic to others, but we can also use the problems we have experienced to inspire us to meet a pressing social need—such as volunteering at a food pantry after dealing with a severe financial struggle, or helping to pass a law that protects childen after facing the traumatic death of a loved one. These acts of service can bring light out of a dark experience, help us to find more meaning in our lives and draw to ourselves the blessings and grace of God.

Blessed and happy is he that ariseth to promote the best interests of the peoples and kindreds of the earth.[102]

Man's merit lieth in service and virtue and not in the pageantry of wealth and riches.[103]

Be generous in prosperity, and thankful in adversity. Be worthy of the trust of thy neighbor, and look upon him with a bright and friendly face. Be a treasure to the poor, an admonisher to the rich, an answerer of the cry of the needy, a preserver of the sanctity of thy pledge. Be fair in thy judgment, and guarded in thy speech. Be unjust to no man, and show all meekness to all men. Be as a lamp unto them that walk in darkness, a joy to the sorrowful, a sea for the thirsty, a haven for the distressed, an upholder and defender of the victim of oppression. Let integrity and uprightness distinguish all thine acts. Be a home for the stranger, a balm to the suffering, a tower of strength for the fugitive. Be eyes to the blind, and a guiding light unto the feet of the erring. Be an ornament to the countenance of truth, a crown to the brow of fidelity, a pillar of the temple of righteousness, a breath of life to the body of mankind, an ensign of the hosts of justice, a luminary above the horizon of virtue, a dew to the soil of the human heart, an ark on the ocean of knowledge, a sun in the heaven of bounty, a gem on the diadem of wisdom, a shining light in the firmament of thy generation, a fruit upon the tree of humility.[104]

Be anxiously concerned with the needs of the age ye live in.[105]

Let your vision be world-embracing, rather than confined to your own self.[106]

What profit is there in agreeing that universal friendship is good, and talking of the solidarity of the human race as a grand ideal? Unless these thoughts are translated into the world of action, they are useless.

The wrong in the world continues to exist just because people talk only of their ideals, and do not strive to put them into practice. If actions took the place of words, the world's misery would very soon be changed into comfort.[107]

Without action nothing in the material world can be accomplished, neither can words unaided advance a man in the spiritual Kingdom. It is not through lip-service only that the elect of God have attained to holiness, but by patient lives of active service they have brought light into the world.

Therefore strive that your actions day by day may be beautiful prayers. Turn towards God, and seek always to do that which is right and noble. Enrich the poor, raise the fallen, comfort the sorrowful, bring healing to the sick, reassure the fearful, rescue the oppressed, bring hope to the hopeless, shelter the destitute![108]

All effort and exertion put forth by man from the fullness of his heart is worship, if it is prompted by the highest motives and the will to do service to humanity. This is worship: to serve mankind and to minister to the needs of the people. Service is prayer.[109]

We should all visit the sick. When they are in sorrow and suffering, it is a real help and benefit to have a friend come. Happiness is a great healer to those who are ill. . . . The people in the East show the utmost kindness and compassion to the sick and suffering. This has greater effect than the remedy itself. You must always have this thought of love and affection when you visit the ailing and afflicted.[110]

Be ye loving fathers to the orphan, and a refuge to the helpless, and a treasury for the poor, and a cure for the ailing. Be ye the helpers of every victim of oppression, the patrons of the disadvantaged. Think ye at all times of rendering some service to every member of the human race. Pay ye no heed to aversion and rejection, to disdain, hostility, injustice: act ye in the opposite way. Be ye sincerely kind, not in appearance only. Let each one of God's loved ones centre his attention on this: to be the Lord's mercy to man; to be the Lord's grace. Let him do some good to every person whose path he crosseth, and be of some benefit to him. Let him improve the character of each and all, and reorient the minds of men.[111]

Nearness to God is possible through devotion to Him, through entrance into the Kingdom and service to humanity; it is attained by unity with mankind and through loving-kindness to all; it is dependent upon investigation of truth, acquisition of praiseworthy virtues, service in the cause of universal peace and personal sanctification.[112]

———•———

Consecrate and devote yourselves to the betterment and service of all the human race. Let no barrier of ill feeling or personal prejudice exist between these souls, for when your motives are universal and your intentions heavenly in character, when your aspirations are centered in the Kingdom, there is no doubt whatever that you will become the recipients of the bounty and good pleasure of God.[113]

———•———

Senses and faculties have been bestowed upon us, to be devoted to the service of the general good; so that we, distinguished above all other forms of life for perceptiveness and reason, should labor at all times and along all lines, whether the occasion be great or small, ordinary or extraordinary, until all mankind are safely gathered into the impregnable stronghold of knowledge. We should continually be establishing new bases for human happiness and creating and promoting new instrumentalities toward this end. How excellent, how honorable is man if he arises to fulfil his responsibilities; how wretched and contemptible, if he shuts his eyes to the welfare of society and wastes his precious life in pursuing his own selfish interests and personal advantages. Supreme happiness is man's, and he beholds the signs of God in the world and in the human soul, if he urges on the steed of high endeavor in the arena of civilization and justice.[114]

Service to the friends is service to the Kingdom of God, and consideration shown to the poor is one of the greatest teachings of God.[115]

For you I desire spiritual distinction—that is, you must become eminent and distinguished in morals. In the love of God you must become distinguished from all else. You must become distinguished for loving humanity, for unity and accord, for love and justice. In brief, you must become distinguished in all the virtues of the human world; for faithfulness and steadfastness, for philanthropic deeds and service to the human world, for love toward every human being, for unity and accord with all people, for removing prejudices and promoting international peace.[116]

Service is the magnet which draws the Divine Confirmations.[117]

SELECTED PRAYERS

Prayer has a great power to help us with the struggles we face in life. Although we may not find that our prayers are answered in the ways we expect, turning our thoughts to our Creator will always help to calm us and put our hearts in touch with our spiritual nature.

Thy name is my healing, O my God, and remembrance of Thee is my remedy. Nearness to Thee is my hope, and love for Thee is my companion. Thy mercy to me is my healing and my succor in both this world and the world to come. Thou, verily, art the All-Bountiful, the All-Knowing, the All-Wise.[1]

O my God! O my God! Unite the hearts of Thy servants, and reveal to them Thy great purpose. May they follow Thy commandments and abide in Thy law. Help them, O God, in their endeavor, and grant them strength to serve Thee. O God! Leave them not to themselves, but guide their steps by the light of Thy knowledge, and cheer their hearts by Thy love. Verily, Thou art their Helper and their Lord.[2]

Dispel my grief by Thy bounty and Thy generosity, O God, my God, and banish mine anguish through Thy sovereignty and Thy might. Thou seest me, O my God, with my face set towards Thee at a time when sorrows have compassed me on every side. I implore Thee, O Thou Who art the Lord of all being, and overshadowest all things visible and invisible, by Thy Name whereby Thou hast subdued the hearts and the souls of men, and by the billows of the Ocean of Thy mercy and the splendors of the Day-Star of Thy bounty, to number me with them whom nothing whatsoever hath deterred from setting their faces toward Thee, O Thou Lord of all names and Maker of the heavens!

Thou beholdest, O my Lord, the things which have befallen me in Thy days. I entreat Thee, by Him Who is the Day-Spring of Thy names and the Dawning-Place of Thine attributes, to ordain for me what will enable me to arise to serve Thee and to extol Thy virtues. Thou art, verily, the Almighty, the Most Powerful, Who art wont to answer the prayers of all men!

And, finally, I beg of Thee by the light of Thy countenance to bless my affairs, and redeem my debts, and satisfy my needs. Thou art He to Whose power and to Whose dominion every tongue hath testified, and Whose majesty and Whose sovereignty every understanding heart hath acknowledged. No God is there but Thee, Who hearest and art ready to answer.[3]

Create in me a pure heart, O my God, and renew a tranquil conscience within me, O my Hope! Through the spirit of power confirm Thou me in Thy Cause, O my Best-Beloved, and by the light of Thy glory reveal unto me Thy path, O Thou the Goal of my desire! Through the power of Thy transcendent might lift me up unto the heaven of Thy holiness, O Source of my being, and by the breezes of Thine eternity gladden me, O Thou Who art my God! Let Thine everlasting melodies breathe tranquility on me, O my Companion, and let the riches of Thine ancient countenance deliver me from all except Thee, O my Master, and let the tidings of the revelation of Thine incorruptible Essence bring me joy, O Thou Who art the most manifest of the manifest and the most hidden of the hidden![4]

If it be Thy pleasure, make me to grow as a tender herb in the meadows of Thy grace, that the gentle winds of Thy will may stir me up and bend me into conformity with Thy pleasure, in such wise that my movement and my stillness may be wholly directed by Thee.[5]

My God, my Adored One, my King, my Desire! What tongue can voice my thanks to Thee? I was heedless, Thou didst awaken me. I had turned back from Thee, Thou didst graciously aid me to turn towards Thee. I was as one dead, Thou didst quicken me with the water of life. I was withered, Thou didst revive me with the heavenly stream of Thine utterance which hath flowed forth from the Pen of the All-Merciful.

O Divine Providence! All existence is begotten by Thy bounty; deprive it not of the waters of Thy generosity, neither do Thou withhold it from the ocean of Thy mercy. I beseech Thee to aid and assist me at all times and under all conditions, and seek from the heaven of Thy grace Thine ancient favor. Thou art, in truth, the Lord of bounty, and the Sovereign of the kingdom of eternity.[6]

I bear witness, O my God, that Thou hast created me to know Thee and to worship Thee. I testify, at this moment, to my powerlessness and to Thy might, to my poverty and to Thy wealth.

There is none other God but Thee, the Help in Peril, the Self-Subsisting.[7]

Is there any Remover of difficulties save God? Say: Praised be God! He is God! All are His servants, and all abide by His bidding![8]

I adjure Thee by Thy might, O my God! Let no harm beset me in times of tests, and in moments of heedlessness guide my steps aright through Thine inspiration. Thou art God, potent art Thou to do what Thou desirest. No one can withstand Thy Will or thwart Thy Purpose.[9]

Lord! Pitiful are we, grant us Thy favor; poor, bestow upon us a share from the ocean of Thy wealth; needy, do Thou satisfy us; abased, give us Thy glory. The fowls of the air and the beasts of the field receive their meat each day from Thee, and all beings partake of Thy care and loving-kindness.

Deprive not this feeble one of Thy wondrous grace and vouchsafe by Thy might unto this helpless soul Thy bounty.

Give us our daily bread, and grant Thine increase in the necessities of life, that we may be dependent on none other but Thee, may commune wholly with Thee, may walk in Thy ways and declare Thy mysteries. Thou art the almighty and the Loving and the Provider of all mankind.[10]

O God! Refresh and gladden my spirit. Purify my heart. Illumine my powers. I lay all my affairs in Thy hand. Thou art my Guide and my Refuge. I will no longer be sorrowful and grieved; I will be a happy and joyful being. O God! I will no longer be full of anxiety, nor will I let trouble harass me. I will not dwell on the unpleasant things of life.

O God! Thou art more friend to me than I am to myself. I dedicate myself to Thee, O Lord.[11]

O God, my God! Shield Thy trusted servants from the evils of self and passion, protect them with the watchful eye of Thy loving-kindness from all rancor, hate and envy, shelter them in the impregnable stronghold of Thy care and, safe from the darts of doubtfulness, make them the manifestations of Thy glorious signs, illumine their faces with the effulgent rays shed from the Dayspring of Thy divine unity, gladden their hearts with the verses revealed from Thy holy kingdom, strengthen their loins by Thine all-swaying power that cometh from Thy realm of glory. Thou art the All-Bountiful, the Protector, the Almighty, the Gracious.[12]

O my Lord! Thou knowest that the people are encircled with pain and calamities and are environed with hardships and trouble. Every trial doth attack man and every dire adversity doth assail him like unto the assault of a serpent. There is no shelter and asylum for him except under the wing of Thy protection, preservation, guard and custody.

O Thou the Merciful One! O my Lord! Make Thy protection my armor, Thy preservation my shield, humbleness before the door of Thy oneness my guard, and Thy custody and defense my fortress and my abode.

Preserve me from the suggestions of self and desire, and guard me from every sickness, trial, difficulty and ordeal.

Verily, Thou art the Protector, the Guardian, the Preserver, the Sufficer, and verily, Thou art the Merciful of the Most Merciful.[13]

NOTES

WHY DO WE HAVE PROBLEMS?

1. 'Abdu'l-Bahá, *Paris Talks*, no. 15.9.
2. 'Abdu'l-Bahá, in *Star of the West* 14, no. 2 (1923): 41.
3. 'Abdu'l-Bahá, *Selections from the Writings of 'Abdu'l-Bahá*, no. 89.1.
4. 'Abdu'l-Bahá, in *Star of the West* 8, no. 19 (1917): 238–39 (new translation attached to letter dated October 10, 1984 from Department of the Secretariat to U.S. Bahá'í Publishing Trust).
5. 'Abdu'l-Bahá, *The Promulgation of Universal Peace*, pp. 225–26.
6. 'Abdu'l-Bahá, *Paris Talks*, no. 18.2–5.
7. Attributed to 'Abdu'l-Bahá, from the diary of Ahmad Sohrab, *Star of the West* 8, no. 18 (1917): 231.
8. Shoghi Effendi, *The World Order of Bahá'u'lláh*, pp. 45–46.
9. On behalf of Shoghi Effendi, in *Unfolding Destiny*, p. 434.
10. On behalf of Shoghi Effendi, in *Lights of Guidance*, no. 2042.
11. Ibid., no 1014.
12. Ibid., no. 2039.
13. Ibid., no. 2049.
14. Bahá'u'lláh, *Gleanings*, no. 128.4.
15. 'Abdu'l-Bahá, *Paris Talks*, no. 35.4–6.
16. 'Abdu'l-Bahá, *Selections from the Writings of 'Abdu'l-Bahá*, no. 170.1.
17. 'Abdu'l-Bahá, *Paris Talks*, no. 57.2.
18. 'Abdu'l-Bahá, *Selections from the Writings of 'Abdu'l-Bahá*, no. 197.1.
19. 'Abdu'l-Bahá, *Paris Talks*, no. 35.3.
20. On behalf of Shoghi Effendi, in *Lights of Guidance*, no. 447.
21. Bahá'u'lláh, *Gleanings*, no. 110.1.
22. Bahá'u'lláh, *Tablets of Bahá'u'lláh*, p. 69.
23. Bahá'u'lláh, Kitáb-i-Íqán, ¶213.
24. Ibid., no. 131.2

25. 'Abdu'l-Bahá, *Paris Talks*, no. 14.2.
26. 'Abdu'l-Bahá, in *Star of the West* 8, no. 18 (1917): 235 (new translation attached to letter dated October 10, 1984 from Department of the Secretariat to U.S. Bahá'í Publishing Trust).
27. On behalf of Shoghi Effendi, in *Lights of Guidance*, no. 391.
28. On behalf of Shoghi Effendi, *Unfolding Destiny*, p. 449.
29. The Universal House of Justice, *Messages from the Universal House of Justice*, no. 126.2.
30. Ibid., no. 126.4.

Where Do Our Problems Come From?

1. Bahá'u'lláh, *Gleanings*, no. 82.1.
2. Bahá'u'lláh, quoted in the Universal House of Justice, *Messages from the Universal House of Justice*, no. 206.3b.
3. Bahá'u'lláh, *Gleanings*, no. 27.2–3.
4. Ibid., no. 109.2.
5. Ibid., no. 43.3.
6. Bahá'u'lláh, *Epistle to the Son of the Wolf*, p. 30.
7. Bahá'u'lláh, quoted in J. E. Esslemont, *Bahá'u'lláh and the New Era*, p. 120.
8. 'Abdu'l-Bahá, *The Secret of Divine Civilization*, p. 59.
9. 'Abdu'l-Bahá, *Selections from the Writings of 'Abdu'l-Bahá*, no. 111.1–3.
10. 'Abdu'l-Bahá, *Some Answered Questions*, no. 75.
11. On behalf of Shoghi Effendi, in *The Compilation of Compilations* 2:11.
12. On behalf of Shoghi Effendi, *Unfolding Destiny*, p. 454.
13. Ibid., p. 453.
14. 'Abdu'l-Bahá, *Selections from the Writings of 'Abdu'l-Bahá*, no. 180.
15. 'Abdu'l-Bahá, *The Promulgation of Universal Peace*, pp. 469–70.
16. 'Abdu'l-Bahá, quoted in a letter written on behalf of the Universal House of Justice, in Brian Kurzius, *Fire and Gold*, pp. 88–89.
17. Attributed to 'Abdu'l-Bahá, in *Star of the West* 8, no. 2 (1917): 25.
18. Attributed to 'Abdu'l-Bahá, in *Star of the West* 6, no. 6 (1915): 44.

19. The Universal House of Justice, *Messages from the Universal House of Justice*, no. 151.5
20. Bahá'u'lláh, Hidden Words, Persian, no. 51.
21. Ibid., no. 53.
22. 'Abdu'l-Bahá, *Selections from the Writings of 'Abdu'l-Bahá*, no. 175.
23. Ibid., no. 176.
24. Ibid., no. 198.5.
25. 'Abdu'l-Bahá, *Paris Talks*, no. 31.9–10.
26. Attributed to 'Abdu'l-Bahá, in *Star of the West* 8, no. 2 (1917): 19.
27. On behalf of Shoghi Effendi, in *Lights of Guidance*, no. 449.
28. Ibid., no. 440.
29. On behalf of the Universal House of Justice, in "A Chaste and Holy Life," *The Compilation of Compilations* vol. 1, no. 138, pp. 53–4.
30. Bahá'u'lláh, quoted in the Universal House of Justice, *Messages from the Universal House of Justice*, no. 246.3.
31. 'Abdu'l-Bahá, *The Promulgation of Universal Peace*, p. 469.
32. 'Abdu'l-Bahá, *Selections from the Writings of 'Abdu'l-Bahá*, no. 39.4.
33. On behalf of Shoghi Effendi, in *Lights of Guidance*, no. 395.
34. Ibid., no. 446.
35. On behalf of the Universal House of Justice, in Brian Kurzius, *Fire and Gold*, p. 123. (Quoted reference is from Bahá'u'lláh, *Gleanings*, no. 131.2.)
36. On behalf of the Universal House of Justice, *Messages from the Universal House of Justice*, no. 246.4.
37. Bahá'u'lláh, *Gleanings*, no. 80.2.
38. 'Abdu'l-Bahá, *Selections from the Writings of 'Abdu'l-Bahá*, no. 132.
39. 'Abdu'l-Bahá, *Paris Talks*, no. 3.2.
40. 'Abdu'l-Bahá, *Selections from the Writings of 'Abdu'l-Bahá*, no. 133.2.
41. Ibid., no. 136.
42. On behalf of Shoghi Effendi, in *Lights of Guidance*, no. 928.
43. On behalf of Shoghi Effendi, in "Selections from the Bahá'í Writings on Some Aspects of Health and Healing," *The Compilation of Compilations* 1:477.

44. On behalf of Shoghi Effendi, in *Lights of Guidance*, no. 948.
45. On behalf of the Universal House of Justice, ibid., no. 955.
46. Ibid., no. 954.
47. Bahá'u'lláh, *Gleanings,* no. 81.
48. 'Abdu'l-Bahá, *Selections from the Writings of 'Abdu'l-Bahá*, no. 169.1–2.
49. 'Abdu'l-Bahá, *The Promulgation of Universal Peace*, p. 47–48.
50. 'Abdu'l-Bahá, *Some Answered Questions,* no. 61.3.
51. 'Abdu'l-Bahá, *Selections from the Writings of 'Abdu'l-Bahá*, no. 149.3–4.
52. 'Abdu'l-Bahá, *Star of the West* 11, no. 15 (1920): 260.
53. 'Abdu'l-Bahá, *'Abdu'l-Bahá in London,* p. 96.
54. Attributed to 'Abdu'l-Bahá, quoted in Lady Blomfield, *The Chosen Highway,* p. 215.
55. On behalf of Shoghi Effendi, in *Lights of Guidance,* no. 697.
56. Ibid., no. 683.

How Can We Cope With Our Problems?

1. Bahá'u'lláh, *Tablets of Bahá'u'lláh,* p. 190.
2. Bahá'u'lláh, Súriy-i-Mulúk ¶65, in *Summons of the Lord of Hosts.*
3. Bahá'u'lláh, in "Fire and Light," *The Bahá'í World* 18:10–11.
4. The Báb, *Selections from the Writings of the Báb,* no. 4.8.1–2.
5. Ibid., no. 3.31.1.
6. 'Abdu'l-Bahá, *The Promulgation of Universal Peace,* p. 448.
7. 'Abdu'l-Bahá, *Selections from the Writings of 'Abdu'l-Bahá,* no. 22.
8. Ibid., no. 178.1.
9. 'Abdu'l-Bahá, *Paris Talks,* no. 34.7–8.
10. Attributed to 'Abdu'l-Bahá, in Marzieh Gail, *Summon up Remembrance,* p. 254.
11. Shoghi Effendi, *Dawn of a New Day,* p. 197.
12. On behalf of Shoghi Effendi, in *Lights of Guidance,* no. 247.
13. On behalf of the Universal House of Justice, in *The Compilation of Compilations* 2:459.

NOTES

14. Bahá'u'lláh, *Gleanings*, no. 34.8.
15. Ibid., no. 77.
16. Ibid., no. 52.2.
17. Bahá'u'lláh, as quoted in J. E. Esslemont, *Bahá'u'lláh and the New Era*, p. 120.
18. 'Abdu'l-Bahá, in *Star of the West* 10, no. 19 (1919): 348.
19. 'Abdu'l-Bahá, *Selections from the Writings of 'Abdu'l-Bahá*, no. 2.15.
20. 'Abdu'l-Bahá, *Paris Talks*, no. 6.7.
21. 'Abdu'l-Bahá, *The Secret of Divine Civilization*, p. 23.
22. 'Abdu'l-Bahá, in *Star of the West* 8, no. 6 (1918): 68.
23. 'Abdu'l-Bahá, *The Promulgation of Universal Peace*, p. 294.
24. 'Abdu'l-Bahá, *Paris Talks*, no. 1.9.
25. 'Abdu'l-Bahá, *The Promulgation of Universal Peace*, pp. 46–48.
26. 'Abdu'l-Bahá, *Selections from the Writings of 'Abdu'l-Bahá*, no. 110.1.
27. Attributed to 'Abdu'l-Bahá, from the diary of Ahmad Sohrab, *Star of the West* 8, no. 1 (1918): 21.
28. Attributed to 'Abdu'l-Bahá, in Juliet Thompson, *The Diary of Juliet Thompson*, p. 21.
29. Ibid., p. 24–25
30. Attributed to 'Abdu'l-Bahá from the diary of Ahmad Sohrab, *Star of the West* 13, no. 6 (1922): 152.
31. Ibid., pp. 270–1.
32. On behalf of Shoghi Effendi, in *Lights of Guidance*, no. 701.
33. Bahá'u'lláh, *Gleanings*, no. 153.8.
34. Bahá'u'lláh, Hidden Words, Arabic, no. 52.
35. 'Abdu'l-Bahá, *Selections from the Writings of 'Abdu'l-Bahá*, no. 150.1–2.
36. Ibid., no. 161.2.
37. Ibid., no. 3.19.
38. Ibid., no. 195.5.
39. Attributed to 'Abdu'l-Bahá, in *Star of the West* 6, no. 6 (1915):45.
40. On behalf of Shoghi Effendi, *Unfolding Destiny*, pp. 459–60.
41. Bahá'u'lláh, *Tablets of Bahá'u'lláh*, p. 138.

42. Bahá'u'lláh, *Gleanings*, no. 66.11.
43. Ibid., no. 153.9.
44. Ibid., no. 134.2.
45. Bahá'u'lláh, *Tablets of Bahá'u'lláh*, p. 155, 156.
46. Ibid., p. 175.
47. Bahá'u'lláh, *The Seven Valleys*, pp. 13–15.
48. Bahá'u'lláh, *Gleanings*, no. 160.2.
49. 'Abdu'l-Bahá, *The Promulgation of Universal Peace*, p. 54.
50. 'Abdu'l-Bahá, *Paris Talks*, no. 35.2.
51. 'Abdu'l-Bahá, in *Star of the West* 14, no. 6 (1923): 168.
52. Ibid., p. 165.
53. 'Abdu'l-Bahá, in Adib Taherzadeh, *The Revelation of Bahá'u'lláh*, 1:100.
54. Attributed to 'Abdu'l-Bahá from the diary of Ahmad Sohrab, in *Star of the West* 8, no. 2 (1917): 17.
55. Shoghi Effendi, *Unfolding Destiny*, p. 456.
56. On behalf of Shoghi Effendi, in *Lights of Guidance*, no. 2046.
57. On behalf of Shoghi Effendi, in "The Individual and Teaching," *The Compilation of Compilations* 2:23.
58. On behalf of Shoghi Effendi, in *Lights of Guidance*, no. 704.
59. Ibid., no. 386.
60. Bahá'u'lláh, in "The Importance of Deepening Our Knowledge and Understanding of the Faith," *The Compilation of Compilations* 1:188.
61. Bahá'u'lláh, *Prayers and Meditations*, no. 55.
62. Bahá'u'lláh, *Gleanings*, no. 136.2.
63. Bahá'u'lláh, in "The Importance of Deepening Our Knowledge and Understanding of the Faith," *The Compilation of Compilations* 1:188.
64. 'Abdu'l-Bahá, *Paris Talks*, nos. 35.8–10.
65. 'Abdu'l-Bahá, in "Crisis and Victory," *The Compilation of Compilations* 1:156.
66. 'Abdu'l-Bahá, *Selections from the Writings of 'Abdu'l-Bahá*, no. 139.7.
67. 'Abdu'l-Bahá, *The Promulgation of Universal Peace*, pp. 246–47.
68. 'Abdu'l-Bahá, *Some Answered Questions*, no. 66.6.

69. Ibid., no. 62.6.
70. 'Abdu'l-Bahá, *Paris Talks,* nos. 54.11–12, 54.14.
71. Ibid., no. 57.4.
72. Attributed to 'Abdu'l-Bahá, quoted in J. E. Esslemont, *Bahá'u'lláh and the New Era,* p. 194.
73. On behalf of Shoghi Effendi, in "Prayer, Meditation, and the Devotional Attitude," *The Compilation of Compilations* 2:240.
74. On behalf of Shoghi Effendi to an individual believer March 18, 1951, U.S. National Bahá'í Archives.
75. On behalf of Shoghi Effendi, in *Lights of Guidance,* no. 381.
76. Ibid., no. 1013.
77. Ibid., no. 927.
78. Attributed to Shoghi Effendi, in *Principles of Bahá'í Administration,* pp. 90–91.
79. On behalf of the Universal House of Justice, in *Lights of Guidance,* no. 955.
80. Bahá'u'lláh, Hidden Words, Persian, no. 66.
81. Bahá'u'lláh, *Epistle to the Son of the Wolf,* p. 55.
82. 'Abdu'l-Bahá, *Selections from the Writings of 'Abdu'l-Bahá,* no. 8.8.
83. Ibid., nos. 144.2, 144.6.
84. Ibid., no. 174.5.
85. 'Abdu'l-Bahá, *The Promulgation of Universal Peace,* p. 453.
86. 'Abdu'l-Bahá, *Selections from the Writings of 'Abdu'l-Bahá,* no. 35.11.
87. 'Abdu'l-Bahá, *Tablets of the Divine Plan,* p. 56.
88. 'Abdu'l-Bahá, *The Promulgation of Universal Peace,* p. 315.
89. 'Abdu'l-Bahá, *Will and Testament,* p. 13.
90. 'Abdu'l-Bahá, *The Promulgation of Universal Peace,* p. 244.
91. 'Abdu'l-Bahá, *Paris Talks,* no. 45.6–10.
92. Attributed to 'Abdu'l-Bahá, in Marzieh Gail, *Summon Up Remembrance,* p. 258.
93. Written of behalf of Shoghi Effendi, in *Lights of Guidance,* no. 741.
94. On behalf of Shoghi Effendi, ibid., no. 1341.

95. Ibid., no. 318.
96. Bahá'u'lláh, *Tablets of Bahá'u'lláh*, p. 168.
97. Bahá'u'lláh, "Consultation," in *The Compilation of Compilations* 1:3.
98. Bahá'u'lláh, quoted in the Universal House of Justice, *Messages from the Universal House of Justice*, no. 438.47.
99. 'Abdu'l-Bahá, in *Lights of Guidance*, no. 588.
100. 'Abdu'l-Bahá, in "Consultation," *The Compilation of Compilations* 1:97.
101. 'Abdu'l-Bahá, ibid., pp. 96–97.
102. Bahá'u'lláh, *Gleanings*, no. 117.
103. Bahá'u'lláh, *Tablets of Bahá'u'lláh*, p. 138.
104. Bahá'u'lláh, *Gleanings*, no. 130.
105. Ibid., no. 106.1.
106. Ibid., no. 43.5.
107. 'Abdu'l-Bahá, *Paris Talks*, nos. 1.9–10.
108. Ibid., nos. 26.6–7.
109. Ibid., no. 55.1.
110. 'Abdu'l-Bahá, *The Promulgation of Universal Peace*, p. 204.
111. 'Abdu'l-Bahá, *Selections from the Writings of 'Abdu'l-Bahá*, no. 1.7.
112. 'Abdu'l-Bahá, *The Promulgation of Universal Peace*, p. 148.
113. Ibid., p. 448.
114. 'Abdu'l-Bahá, *The Secret of Divine Civilization*, p. 3.
115. 'Abdu'l-Bahá, *Selections from the Writings of 'Abdu'l-Bahá*, no. 11.
116. 'Abdu'l-Bahá, *The Promulgation of Universal Peace*, p. 190.
117. On behalf of Shoghi Effendi, in *Lights of Guidance*, no. 405

Selected Prayers

1. Bahá'u'lláh, *Prayers and Meditations*, no. 170.
2. Bahá'u'lláh, in *Bahá'í Prayers*, p. 238.
3. Bahá'u'lláh, *Prayers and Meditations*, no. 154.
4. Ibid., no. 155.

5. Ibid., no. 150.2.
6. Ibid., no. 173.
7. Ibid., no. 181.
8. The Báb, in *Bahá'í Prayers*, p. 226.
9. Ibid., p. 227.
10. 'Abdu'l-Bahá, ibid., p. 22.
11. Ibid., p. 174
12. Ibid., pp. 135–36.
13. Ibid., pp. 136.

BIBLIOGRAPHY

Works of Bahá'u'lláh

Epistle to the Son of the Wolf. Translated by Shoghi Effendi. 1st pocket-sized ed. Wilmette, IL: Bahá'í Publishing Trust, 1988.
Gleanings from the Writings of Bahá'u'lláh. Translated by Shoghi Effendi. Wilmette, IL: Bahá'í Publishing, 2005.
The Hidden Words of Bahá'u'lláh. Translated by Shoghi Effendi. Wilmette, IL: Bahá'í Publishing, 2002.
Kitáb-i-Íqán: The Book of Certitude. Translated by Shoghi Effendi. Wilmette, IL: Bahá'í Publishing, 2003.
Prayers and Meditations. Translated by Shoghi Effendi. 1st pocket-sized ed. Wilmette, IL: Bahá'í Publishing Trust, 1987.
The Summons of the Lord of Hosts: Tablets of Bahá'u'lláh. Wilmette, IL: Bahá'í Publishing, 2006.

Works of the Báb

Selections from the Writings of the Báb. Compiled by the Research Department of the Universal House of Justice. Translated by Habib Taherzadeh et al. 1st pocket-sized ed. Wilmette, IL: Bahá'í Publishing Trust, 2006.

Works of 'Abdu'l-Bahá

Paris Talks: Addresses Given by 'Abdu'l-Bahá in Paris in 1911. Wilmette, IL: Bahá'í Publishing Trust, 2006.
The Promulgation of Universal Peace: Talks Delivered by 'Abdu'l-Bahá during His Visit to the United States and Canada in 1912. Compiled by Howard MacNutt. Wilmette, IL: Bahá'í Publishing Trust, 2007.

The Secret of Divine Civilization. Translated by Marzieh Gail and Ali-Kuli Khan. 1st pocket-sized ed. Wilmette, IL: Bahá'í Publishing Trust, 1990.

Selections from the Writings of 'Abdu'l-Bahá. Compiled by the Research Department of the Universal House of Justice. Translated by a Committee at the Bahá'í World Center and by Marzieh Gail. 1st pocket-sized ed. Wilmette, IL: Bahá'í Publishing Trust, 1996.

Some Answered Questions. Compiled and translated by Laura Clifford Barney. 1st pocket-sized ed. Wilmette, IL: Bahá'í Publishing Trust, 2004.

Tablets of the Divine Plan: Revealed by 'Abdu'l-Bahá to the North American Bahá'ís. 1st pocket-sized ed. Wilmette, IL: Bahá'í Publishing Trust, 1993.

Works of Shoghi Effendi

Dawn of a New Day: Messages to India, 1923–1957. New Delhi: Bahá'í Publishing Trust, n.d.

Principles of Bahá'í Administration: A Compilation. 4th ed. London: Bahá'í Publishing Trust, 1973.

The Unfolding Destiny of the British Bahá'í Community: The Messages from the Guardian of the Bahá'í Faith to the Bahá'ís of the British Isles. London: Bahá'í Publishing Trust, 1981.

The World Order of Bahá'u'lláh: Selected Letters. New ed. Wilmette, IL: Bahá'í Publishing Trust, 1991.

Works of the Universal House of Justice

Messages from the Universal House of Justice, 1963–1986: The Third Epoch of the Formative Age. Compiled by Geoffry Marks. Wilmette, IL: Bahá'í Publishing Trust, 1996.

Compilations of Bahá'í Writings

Bahá'u'lláh, the Báb, and 'Abdu'l-Bahá. *Bahá'í Prayers: A Selection of Prayers Revealed by Bahá'u'lláh, the Báb, and 'Abdu'l-Bahá.* New ed. Wilmette, IL: Bahá'í Publishing Trust, 1991.

Hornby, Helen, comp. *Lights of Guidance: A Bahá'í Reference File.* 6th ed. New Delhi: Bahá'í Publishing Trust, 1999.

Kurzius, Brian. *Fire and Gold: Benefitting from Life's Tests.* Oxford: George Ronald, 1995.

The Compilation of Compilations: Prepared by the Universal House of Justice, 1963–1990. 2 vols. Australia: Bahá'í Publications Australia, 1991.

Other Works

The Bahá'í World: An International Record, vol. 18 (1979–1983). Compiled by the Universal House of Justice. Haifa: The Universal House of Justice. 1986.

Blomfield, Lady (Sitárih Khánum). *The Chosen Highway.* Wilmette, IL: Bahá'í Publishing Trust, n.d.; repr. 1975.

Esslemont, J. E. *Bahá'u'lláh and the New Era.* Wilmette, IL: Bahá'í Publishing, 2006.

Gail, Marzieh. *Summon Up Remembrance.* Oxford: George Ronald, 1987.

Taherzadeh, Adib. *The Revelation of Bahá'u'lláh: Baghdad 1853–63.* Oxford: George Ronald, 1974.

Thompson, Juliet. *The Diary of Juliet Thompson.* Los Angeles: Kalimat Press, 1983.

INDEX

A
abasement
  finite, 73
acceptance, 77
action
  need for, 66–67, 107–8
  worship and, 108
afflictions. *See* tests
afterlife
  bliss and joy of, 52
  no time or sunrise in, 54–55
  safe approach to God, 15
American civil war, 11–12
anger
  effects of, 28

B
beauty and youth
  fleeting, 38
beloved of the Lord, 64

C
calamities
  reasons for, 17
children
  suffering of, 34
  training of, 68–69
compassion, 103
confidence, 57, 58, 60

consultation, 102–4
contention
  wrongness of both sides, 98
contentment, 76, 77, 81–82, 83

D
death
  caged bird analogy, 53
  candle analogy, 54
  difficult to welcome, 52
  divine wisdom of, 50–51
  shrub analogy, 54
  similar to birth, 51–52, 53–54
decadent society
  signs of, 41
desire
  devouring fire of, 29
detachment, 72
determination, 63
difficulties. *See* tests
disasters
  natural and man-made, 41
discipline, 63

E
ego
  animalistic, 31–32
  subordination of, 31

enemies
   recognition of as friends, 96–97

F
failure
   means of purifying spirit, 14
faith, 57, 58, 61–62
faithfulness, 111
faults
   overlooking, 95–96, 99
forgiveness, 95–96, 98

G
generosity, 76
God
   answerer of prayers, 86–88
   father, 21
   healing of, 47, 82, 85, 86
   justice of, 63
   love of, 98
   mercy of, 88
   power of, 59
   remover of difficulties, 117
   sufficeth all things, 59
   teacher, 21
   will of, 67–68, 82, 83
   wisdom of, 58–59, 88
gratitude, 76

H
healing
   prayer alone not sufficient, 92–93
   spiritual and physical, 47, 49
health
   safeguarding, 92
helping others
   key to true happiness, 15
human reality
   spiritual in nature, 5
humility
   virtues of, 28

I
ignorance
   root cause of wrongdoing, 29–30
illness
   means of spiritual growth, 11
   mental, 48
   spiritual and physical causes, 46–47
   unavoidable, 46
individual
   aim in life, 35–36
   can change behavior, 62
   development of, 8–10
   happiness of, 65
   responsible for own life, 102
   two natures of, 6, 10

J
jealousy
   reasons to avoid, 28
joy, 18, 76–77, 81
justice, 111

INDEX

K
Kingdom
  real world, 73–74
  world of lights, 9

L
laws
  spiritual, 22
  three types of, 18–19
life
  mortal pilgrimage of, 52
  purpose of, 22–23
  struggle of, 31
love
  potent elixir, 101
  toward every human being, 111–12
lover and the watchman, the, 78–80

M
man
  as "unripe," 17
  exertions determine success, 63, 69
  love for God, 101
  love of toward others, 99
  outlook on life materialistic, 40
  purpose of creation of, 27–28
  reality of, 27
  relationship with God, 65–66
  two natures of, 70

Manifestations of God. *See* Prophets of God
material world
  cause of problems, 36–37
  contrasts of, 81
  darkness in, 43, 74
  disheartenment of, 38–39
  illusion, 16, 72
  inconstancy of, 42–43
  mirage, 73
  no comfort in, 16
  organic unit, 43
  reliance on, 67–68
  sorrow of, 52
  unawareness of God, 15
  vain, empty, 72
materialism
  effects of, 40–41
meditation
  blessings of, 85–86, 89
misery
  grief, sorrow cause of, 64
moderation
  benefits of, 19–20

N
nature
  world of, 32–33

O
ordeals
  two kinds of, 20

P

pain, 12–13, 18
patience, 76, 83
poverty, 37
prayer, 85
   after death, 89
   attitude of true worshipper, 91
   contentment, 116
   divine wisdom and, 91
   effects of, 86, 113
   five steps of, 93–94
   gratitude, 116
   grief, 114–15
   happiness, 118
   healing, 87, 113
   humility, 117–18
   influence of, 90
   Prophet of God and, 92
   protection, 119–20
   purity of heart, 115
   removal of difficulties, 117
   unity, 113
pride
   danger of, 28
prisoner, advice to, 21–22
Prophets of God
   not exempt from suffering, 14, 75, 83
   reason for being sent, 33–34
   reveal spiritual laws, 22
prosperity
   finite, 73
purgation
   stage of man's development, 18

R

religion
   impregnable stronghold, 42
   purpose of, 71–72
   value of, 71

S

sacrifice
   meaning of, 84
saint
   definition of, 32
searching
   for God, 21
   for ourselves, 21
self
   greatest prison, 82
self-surrender, 80
service
   blessings of, 105, 110, 112
   guidance for, 105–6, 109
   nearness to God and, 109–10
   poor and, 111
   prayer and, 108
   reasons for, 110–11
   spiritual distinction and, 111–12
   visits to sick, 108–9
sickness. *See* illness
silence
   true safety, 78
soul
   indefinite journey of, 84
   nobility, beauty of, 55
   progress after death, 49–50, 56, 89

sign of God, 26
unaffected by illness, 45
speech
    joy-giving, 35–36
spirituality
    need for, 40
steadfastness
    blessings of, 76
    need for, 69–70
    spiritual distinction and, 111
success, 84
suffering
    cause of spiritual advancement, 17
    caused by others, 32
    caused by ourselves, 25–26
    principal cause of, 36

T
tests
    gifts of God, 62
    means of growth, 13
    measurement of soul, 75
    prayer and effort solutions, 94
    reasons for, 6–7, 17

thoughts, 65
tongue
    force of, 20
torment
    two kinds of, 30
troubles
    finite nature of, 13
true happiness, 61

U
unity of humankind, 43–44

V
virtues, 77

W
wealth
    barrier to God, 37
    effects of, 39–40
womb
    world of, 8
work
    praiseworthiness of, 78
    source of human happiness, 71

Bahá'í PUBLISHING
and the Bahá'í Faith

Bahá'í Publishing produces books based on the teachings of the Bahá'í Faith. Founded more than 160 years ago, the Bahá'í Faith has spread to some 235 nations and territories and is now accepted by more than five million people. The word "Bahá'í" means "follower of Bahá'u'lláh." Bahá'u'lláh, the founder of the Bahá'í Faith, asserted that he is the Messenger of God for all of humanity in this day. The cornerstone of his teachings is the establishment of the spiritual unity of humankind, which will be achieved by personal transformation and the application of clearly identified spiritual principles. Bahá'ís also believe that there is but one religion and that all the Messengers of God—among them Abraham, Zoroaster, Moses, Krishna, Buddha, Jesus, and Muḥammad—have progressively revealed its nature. Together, the world's great religions are expressions of a single, unfolding divine plan. Human beings, not God's Messengers, are the source of religious divisions, prejudices, and hatreds.

The Bahá'í Faith is not a sect or denomination of another religion, nor is it a cult or a social movement. Rather, it is a globally recognized independent world religion founded on new books of scripture revealed by Bahá'u'lláh.

Bahá'í Publishing is an imprint of the National Spiritual Assembly of the Bahá'ís of the United States.

For more information about the Bahá'í Faith,
or to contact the Bahá'ís near you, visit

http://www.bahai.us/

or call

1-800-22-UNITE

OTHER BOOKS AVAILABLE
FROM BAHÁ'Í PUBLISHING

THE ASCENT OF SOCIETY
The Social Imperative in Personal Salvation
JOHN S. HATCHER
$19.95 U.S. / $22.95 CAN
Trade Paper
978-1-931847-52-0

An illuminating examination of the relationship between individual spiritual development and the collective advancement of civilization.

In *The Purpose of Physical Reality* Dr. John S. Hatcher compared the physical world to a classroom designed by God to stimulate individual spiritual growth and to prepare us for birth into a spiritual existence. But how does personal spiritual development translate into social experience? Is there a social imperative connected with individual spiritual growth? Is involvement with others necessary for one to evolve spiritually? Hatcher analyzes these questions and more in *The Ascent of Society: The Social Imperative in Personal Salvation.* This penetrating study describes the objective of personal spiritual growth as an "ever-expanding sense of self" that requires social relationships in order to develop. Hatcher focuses on the Bahá'í belief that human history is a divinely guided process in which spiritual principles are gradually and progressively expressed in social institutions. He demonstrates that the aspirant to spiritual transformation cannot view personal health and development as being possible apart from the progress of human society as a whole.

John S. Hatcher holds a BA and an MA in English literature from Vanderbilt University and a PhD in English literature from the University of Georgia. He is the director of graduate studies in English literature at the University of South Florida, Tampa. A widely published poet and distinguished lecturer, he has written numerous books on literature, philosophy, and Bahá'í theology and scripture, including *Close Connections: The Bridge between Spiritual and Physical Reality, From the Auroral Darkness: The Life and Poetry of Robert E. Hayden, A Sense of History: The Poetry of John Hatcher, The Ocean of His Words: A Reader's Guide to the Art of Bahá'u'lláh,* and *The Purpose of Physical Reality.* He and his family live on a farm near Plant City, Florida.

RELIGION ON THE HEALING EDGE
What Bahá'ís Believe
FRANK STETZER
$11.95 U.S. / $14.95 CAN
Trade Paper
978-1-931847-44-5

An introduction to the Bahá'í Faith that challenges readers to view religion, civilization, and spirituality in a new way.

Religion on the Healing Edge: What Bahá'ís Believe examines the defining beliefs animating the Bahá'í Faith and its distinctive practices, which are intended to change the world. Author

Frank Stetzer offers insights into the Bahá'í community and its vision to establish a new global civilization based on the recognition of the oneness of humanity. The vision he presents is a bold and audacious one, full of unique opportunities and unusual challenges. A marvelous book for anyone interested in learning more about the mission of the Bahá'í Faith and the relevance of its teachings.

Frank Stetzer is a research statistician in the College of Nursing at the University of Wisconsin-Milwaukee. He holds a PhD in geography and an MS in statistics from the University of Iowa. Dr. Stetzer encountered the Bahá'í religion as a college student in the 1970s. He and his wife, Rosemary, have served in various capacities in several Bahá'í communities. They live in Wisconsin and enjoy the company of their three children.

THE SECRET OF DIVINE CIVILIZATION
'ABDU'L-BAHÁ
$9.95 U.S. / $12.95 CAN
978-1-931847-51-3

An outstanding treatise on the social and spiritual progress both of nations and of individuals.

The Secret of Divine Civilization is a thorough explanation of the view of the Bahá'í Faith on the true nature of civilization. It contains an appealing and universal message inspiring world-mindedness and soliciting the highest human motives and attributes for the establishment of a spiritual society. Written by 'Abdu'l-Bahá in the late nineteenth century as a letter to the rulers and people of Persia, it is still profoundly relevant today as a guide to creating a peaceful and productive world.

'Abdu'l-Bahá, meaning in Arabic "Servant of the Glory," was the title assumed by 'Abbás Effendi (1844–1921), the eldest son and appointed successor of Bahá'u'lláh, the Prophet and Founder of the Bahá'í Faith. A prisoner since the age of nine, 'Abdu'l-Bahá shared a lifetime of imprisonment and exile with his father at the hands of the Ottoman Empire. He spent his entire life in tireless service to, and promotion of, Bahá'u'lláh's teachings.

A WAY OUT OF THE TRAP
A Ten-Step Program for Spiritual Growth
NATHAN RUTSTEIN
$10.95 U.S. / $13.95 CAN
Trade Paper
978-1-931847-40-7

An easy-to-follow guide for people of all faiths to reconnect with God and live more fulfilling lives.

A Way Out of the Trap: A Ten-Step Program for Spiritual Growth offers a process by which the spiritually hungry can find the faith, hope, and spiritual sustenance needed to break out of the trap of hopelessness. Author Nathan Rutstein outlines a spiritual path that can help people of all faiths to reconnect with God. The result is a practical guide to understanding the purpose of life and how to live it.

Author, lecturer, college educator, and former network journalist, Nathan Rutstein has written numerous books about life, spirituality, racism, education, and the oneness of humanity. He is also one of the founders of the Institute for the Healing of Racism in the United States, lecturing at scores of colleges, universities and government institutions on the subject.

To view our complete catalog, please visit
http://books.bahai.us